Gizzi's SEASON'S EATINGS

MITCHELL BEAZLEY

Gizzi's SEASON'S EATINGS

Feasts & Celebrations
FROM HALLOWEEN TO HAPPY NEW YEAR

GIZZI ERSKINE

An Hachette UK Company
www.hachette.co.uk

First published in Great Britain in 2016
by Mitchell Beazley, a division of
Octopus Publishing Group Ltd
Carmelite House
50 Victoria Embankment
London EC4Y 0DZ
www.octopusbooks.co.uk

For Edie
For believing in the
magic like I do
and keeping it alive
in our home.

ISBN 978 1 78472 215 9

A CIP catalogue record for this book
is available from the British Library.

Printed and bound in China

10 9 8 7 6 5 4 3 2 1

Publishing Director Stephanie Jackson
Managing Editor Sybella Stephens
Copy Editor Annie Lee
Creative Director Jonathan Christie
Art Director and Designer Anita Mangan
Photographer Emma Lee
Home Economist and Stylist Emily Ezekiel
Senior Production Manager Peter Hunt

CONTENTS

INTRODUCTION

The whole focus of this book has been to look at the way we embrace eating during the winter season, from October all the way through to the New Year. In some ways this has been one of the more difficult books I've written, as these seasonal celebrations mean the world to me – I find them completely cathartic. They offer me the chance to escape from the harsh reality of the everyday, and allow me (temporarily at least) to skip back to a more innocent time. I just can't help but jump headfirst into them, using as many clichés as possible, decking the halls with holly as I go! All these festivities are based on traditions and I am not out to change these... merely see how they have developed through the years and to add my own twists. The challenge for me has been knowing that so many people feel the same way as I do about this time of year and making sure that my recipes live up to expectations!

There is a common misconception that our seasonal festivities are Americanisms that we've adopted in the UK over the past century, but that's not the case. Most of these celebrations have Pagan and European roots. I wanted to explore each of these festivities, not JUST as an excuse for a shindig, but to understand what they are really about; to look into their history, look into MY history, and piece together why we do what we do. To look at what food produce is sprouting up at this time of the year, and with a healthy dose of merriment and joviality bring them to life with timeless recipes. These are among the few occasions that we seem to be unified – it doesn't matter what religion you are nowadays, these celebrations are invaluable opportunities to come together in an increasingly isolated world.

Let's take Halloween for example. It was always a big deal for me, maybe more than Christmas at times. I was an ethereal child who loved magic and was probably a little "dark" for my age – I would be in the back seat of the car, staring into the sky looking for witches on broomsticks. There was an ominous feeling of fear in the air. Perhaps I lacked a little understanding about what Halloween was really about, but I loved the ghost stories and thrived a little on being frightened. My old school friend Caroline was American and would host a party every year. We would be greeted at her house with the smell of sticky doughnuts and roasted pumpkin seeds, and spend the evening trick-or-treating, bobbing for apples and trying not to lick our lips while eating ring-doughnuts on strings. It's one of those memories where, if I close my eyes, I can almost taste all that sugariness.

Bonfire night would come a week later, then Thanksgiving, or the way we played it in this country, Harvest Festival, which taught us how to be giving, and was a way to understand about agriculture from an early age. Regardless of the event, food would always be found at its epicentre.

When I was a kid I had this magical book that was about Christmas and I lost it. It was the true essence of Christmas without any marketing or Martha Stewart. Every year I would open this book at about the same time as I went back to school in September, in anticipation of the coming season. I hated school, but I loved that going-back-to-school feeling; buying a new pencil case and bag and having squeaky, shiny new shoes. I loved splashing in puddles and coming home really freezing cold, painfully so, to a warm house that smelt of cooking and hot chocolate. I want this book to be that magical book for you. I want this to be the book you return to year upon year, a trusty friend to guide you through these winter celebrations. I want to take the stress out of any gathering you might be hosting, while focusing on seasonal ingredients. This is not a book about healthy eating, this is a book about indulgence and bringing people together.

Halloween is the first opportunity to combine the celebration of the turning of the seasons with folkloric traditions, some of which stretch back to ancient times. We consider Halloween to be an American tradition but, in fact, its roots are ingrained in Paganism from the British Isles. Marked on October 31st, the origins of Halloween date back as far as 2,000 years ago, to the ancient Celtic festival of Samhain (meaning "summer's end") and served to mark the beginning of winter.

For some it was also seen as a time when the boundary between this world and the Otherworld became blurred. Huge sacred bonfires were lit to appease the spirits and fairies wandering the earth. Incantations and charms were thought to be particularly powerful at this time, with the focus on seeking signs for the future to help guide through the long, dark winter. Animal sacrifices, and offerings of food and drink, were commonplace. By around 43AD, the Romans had conquered most of the Celtic territory in Europe, and began amalgamating the Pagan festivals with their own. One of these celebrated Pomona, the goddess of orchards and harvest, who was symbolized by the apple. This may explain the origin of apple bobbing, a tradition which later evolved into a game to predict the marriage prospects of the young. Whoever nabbed a bite of the apple first would be the next to get hitched!

By the 8th century, Pope Gregory III had designated November 1st as All Saint's Day to mark the honouring of saints and martyrs, followed by All Soul's Day on November 2nd to commemorate the dead, that incorporated the more Pagan traditions of the Celts and Romans. October 31st was named All Hallows' Eve, which was later contracted to "Halloween". Trick or treating is closely linked to the All Saint's Day practice of offering ale, food or money to young men travelling from door to door singing "souling" songs. Another tradition was to hand out spiced biscuits called soul cakes to poorer citizens during All Soul's Day parades, which replaced the ancient practice of leaving food and wine outside your door for the roaming souls of loved ones.

Dressing up in costumes initially began as a way to avoid being recognized by wandering ghosts, in the hope of being mistaken as a fellow spirit so as not to encounter any trouble!

Pumpkin carving is an iconic symbol of Halloween, and originated from Ireland where potatoes and turnips were carved into jack-o'-lanterns and set on windowsills to ward off harmful spirits. The introduction of pumpkins to Europe is an example of our traditions being developed by settlers in the US, who also meshed their seasonal customs with those of the Native Americans.

As we move through to the 20th century, America took the lead in turning Halloween into the modern incarnation that we recognize today. Much of this developed after World War II, when the focus began leaning more towards children and bringing communities together through activities such as trick-or-treating. In recent years this has become more popular in the UK too, and it can be a lovely way of getting to know the people in your neighbourhood better.

In this chapter I've taken inspiration from the history of Halloween, while focusing on all the wonderful produce available at this time of year. From a spiced cider that's filled with buttery pan-roasted spooky-faced apples bobbing around, to a big pie filled to the brim with coq au vin in a playful nod to the jack-o'-lantern, there are lots of fun recipes that are great for making with the kids, but also plenty of rich and warming food to fend off the heebie jeebies!

Devilish
delights

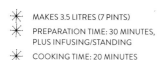
SHRUNKEN HEAD APPLES IN SPICED CIDER

In this recipe you are just making mulled cider really, but if you want to make it extra spooky and pretty cool and are up for flexing your creative muscles, this is a pretty radical way to show off. (See photograph on pages 10–11).

3 litres (5¼ pints) cloudy cider

500ml (18fl oz) cloudy apple juice

3 tablespoons caster sugar

pared zest and juice from 2 oranges

2 cinnamon sticks

2 star anise

6 cloves

12 black peppercorns

2 allspice berries

3 cardamom pods

2 bay leaves

100ml (3½fl oz) Calvados or brandy (optional, but do have it if you like it boozy)

For the shrunken head apples

5 Cox's apples

juice of 2 lemons

1 tablespoon caster sugar

2 tablespoons unsalted butter

Peel your apples and place them in very cold water with the squeezed-out lemons.

Meanwhile get your mulled cider going. There is an argument about whether to put the aromatics in a mulling bag, which you can buy from good kitchen shops, or leave them loose in the pan – I like to leave them in the pan as they look rather beautiful floating around but it is, I suppose, more practical to package them up. If you can't find mulling bags, wrap the spices in some muslin and make a bundle, tying it with kitchen string.

Place the cider, juice, sugar, orange peel, spices and bay leaves in a very large pan. Bring it slowly to the boil, but do not let it actually boil – this will take 10–15 minutes. Switch off the heat and allow all the flavours to infuse the cider for a further 15 minutes, then add the Calvados or brandy (if using).

To make the shrunken head apples, peel the apples, then carefully carve them into spooky faces with a sharp knife or a craft knife. It's easier than it sounds – be creative! The apples will spin around in the cider, so I recommend carving 2 faces on each apple.

Heat the butter and caster sugar in a small pan and, when it's really hot and foaming, pan-fry the apple faces to brown them, as this will bring out the detail in the faces. (You may find it easier to do this in batches.) When the apples have browned, tip them, butter and all, into the cider. Reheat the cider to just under boiling point, then turn off the heat and it's ready to serve by ladling into mugs. The apples are delicious to eat afterwards for pudding, with cream.

PUMPKIN PURÉE

✳ MAKES 450G (1LB) PURÉE
✳ PREPARATION TIME: 15 MINUTES
✳ COOKING TIME: 25 MINUTES

Autumn is pumpkin season, and many recipes in this book, from the pumpkin gnocchi to the pumpkin pie, use pumpkin purée as a base. It's great just to have to hand during the autumnal months and makes a super side for so many dishes. It can also be thinned out to make a brilliant soup.

500g (1lb 2oz) orange pumpkin, any variety you like

30g (1oz) unsalted butter

Peel the pumpkin and cut it into 1cm (½ inch) chunks. Heat the butter in a large pan and throw in the pumpkin. Cook very gently over a low heat with a lid on, stirring every so often, for 20 minutes or until the pumpkin is cooked through. The closed pan will both steam and pan-cook the pumpkin with no effort, but towards the end of the cooking process, really scrape away at the bottom of the pan to avoid it catching and burning, as pumpkin contains a lot of sugar.

When the pumpkin is cooked all the way through, place in a high-powered blender and blitz until smooth. Store in a plastic container in the fridge for up to 5 days, or leave to cool and use straight away.

MAKING ROASTED PUMPKIN SEEDS

✳ MAKES AS MANY AS YOU HAVE
✳ PREPARATION TIME: 10 MINUTES, PLUS COOLING
✳ COOKING TIME: 10 MINUTES

leftover pumpkin seeds

olive oil

sea salt flakes

flavourings of your choice, such as finely chopped rosemary, chilli powder, ground cumin or brown sugar (optional)

When you have cleaned out your pumpkin you will have loads of seeds – don't throw them away! First clean them really well, pull off the stringy bits of pumpkin flesh, then rinse them and dry on kitchen paper.

Preheat the oven to 220°C/200°C fan (425°F), Gas Mark 7. Spread the seeds evenly over a baking tray, then drizzle with olive oil and salt. You can play with other ingredients here too, such as one of the suggested flavourings. Make sure the seeds are well coated, then roast for 10 minutes. Leave to cool for 15 minutes before serving.

COQ AU VIN
SPOOKY-FACED PIE

A really good pie is filled with a really good stew. The best of chicken stews is the coq au vin. It beats a white sauce-filled pie any day of the week, but I rarely see it used as a pie filling. The truth is, though, that this pie is as much about the filling as it is about using the pie lid to make a really cool Halloween-y spooky face. It's the ultimate Halloween crowd-pleaser, and this recipe makes a mammoth pie that will easily feed 8 people. I am a believer in a real pie, not a lidded puff pastry pot pie (they send me into a fury). I would serve this with mash and Really Simple Honey Glazed Carrots & Parsnips (see page 186).

For the stew

2 tablespoons rapeseed oil

12 free-range chicken thighs, boned, skinned and halved (if you're not sure about removing bones or skin, just ask your butcher to do it)

300g (10½oz) button chestnut mushrooms

8 thick smoked streaky bacon rashers, chopped into thin lardons

12 small shallots or baby white onions

4 garlic cloves, peeled but left whole

1 tablespoon tomato purée

2 tablespoons plain flour

600ml (20fl oz) red wine (use a full-bodied one like Bordeaux)

500ml (18fl oz) chicken stock

1 bouquet garni, made with bay leaves, thyme and parsley, tied in a bundle

2 teaspoons sugar

2 tablespoons sherry or red wine vinegar

sea salt flakes and freshly ground black pepper

For the pie

plain flour, for dusting

2 x 375g (13oz) packets of all-butter shortcrust pastry

1 free-range egg, beaten (for the glaze)

Heat the oven to 200°C/180°C fan (400°F), Gas Mark 6.

Heat 1 tablespoon of the oil in a large heavy-based, lidded casserole dish. Season the chicken thighs with salt and pepper and brown them in 2 batches until all sides are golden brown. Throw in the mushrooms, cook in the oil and chicken juices for 5 minutes, or until golden, and set aside with the chicken. If the bottom of the pan seems dry, add a little boiling water and scrape the goodness from the bottom of the pan.

Add the remaining oil to the pan and cook the bacon over a high heat for 2 minutes. Reduce the heat, add the shallots or baby onions and garlic, and pan-fry for 4–5 minutes. Add the tomato purée and stir to coat for a minute, then add the flour and cook for a further minute.

Slowly pour in the wine, stirring continuously to emulsify the sauce (you'll see it thicken up as you stir). Add the chicken stock, chicken thighs, mushrooms and bouquet garni, then give it a good stir! Cover, place in the oven and cook for 1 hour, stirring it halfway through cooking. When the time is up, remove the bundle of herbs, then season with salt and pepper and also with a clever little thing called a gastrique. To make this, in a small pan melt the sugar with the vinegar and bring to the boil. Your kitchen will reek, but this elixir will bring your stew to the next level. Pour it into the stew and stir it in, let it cool to room temperature, then put it in the fridge overnight.

RECIPE CONTINUED OVERLEAF

COQ AU VIN
SPOOKY-FACED PIE *CONT...*

When you're ready to make your pie, dust your kitchen surface with flour, then roll out one of the blocks of pastry and use it to line the base of a 23cm (9 inch) pie dish, making sure the pastry hangs over the edge. At this stage, do not trim the edges. Fill the pie with the fridge-cold pie filling. Using a pastry brush, glaze the edges of the pastry with the beaten egg. Roll out the other block of pastry to make the top, then dust your rolling pin with flour and fold the pastry over it. Roll the lid of the pastry off the pin and over the edges of the base. Now trim off the excess pastry to make a neat edge. You can push down the edges with a fork to seal them tight, but I prefer to use the 'crimping method', which uses one finger to push the pastry down towards the outside of the dish. Pinch around that finger with the finger and thumb of your other hand to create a scalloped effect.

With a small sharp knife, cut out a spooky face pattern in the pastry, then brush with the beaten egg glaze and put into the fridge to chill for 30 minutes.

Meanwhile, heat the oven to 220°C/200°C fan (425°F), Gas Mark 7.

Glaze the top of the pie once more, then bake for 35–40 minutes, or until the pastry is golden brown and cooked all the way through, and the filling is bubbling.

Halloween pumpkins

SPOOKY PUMPKIN LANTERN

You will need:

1 HUGE Pumpkin

a marker pen

pumpkin cutters or a thin sharp knife

a spoon

tea lights

I find it's easiest to draw the design of your scary face on to the pumpkin with a marker pen before you start. Draw holes for the eyes, nose, mouth, or whatever you fancy!

Cut out a lid at the top of the pumpkin by inserting a sharp knife in a circle around the stalk. Lift this out, then scoop out all of the seeds and gubbins with a spoon until the inside is empty (save the seeds to make Roasted Pumpkin Seeds, see page 13). Now you are ready to carve out the eyes, nose and mouth. Take your time with this, and be sure to supervise any young children. Another nice thing to do is just carve the skin away in a pattern without cutting through the flesh, as this will glow orange once the pumpkin is illuminated. Once you've finished your design, light a tea light and carefully place inside. Put the lid back on to prevent the candle from going out.

PRETTY PUMPKIN LANTERNS

You will need:

a variety of pumpkins in different sizes

pumpkin cutters or a thin sharp knife

a spoon

a marker pen

a hand drill or electric drill

tea lights

Take your pumpkin and cut out a lid and scoop out the seeds in the same way as the Spooky Pumpkin Lantern (see above), but instead of drawing a face on the front, draw dot patterns all over the entire pumpkin. Try not to make them too close together. You can do this in a geometric way, or even draw something special like a collection of stars.

Next take your drill and drill out the holes to build up the pattern. Use a drill bit that's not too fine, but also not too large, or alternatively use a variety of different-sized drill bits.

Once you've finished your design, light a tea light and carefully place inside. Put the lid back on to prevent the candle from going out.

GLITTER PUMPKINS

You will need:

a variety of pumpkins or gourds in
 different sizes

acrylic paint, any colour you like but it
 must match your glitter

a paint brush

glitter

PVA glue

Paint your pumpkins with the acrylic paint and leave to dry.

To make the acrylic glitter, simply mix your glitter with the PVA glue until your glue is thick with glitter but still the consistency of paint. Brush the glitter glue over the entire pumpkins – this will turn translucent when it dries. You may decide to do two coats depending on how glittery you want your pumpkins. Allow ample time to dry in a ventilated area.

CAT PUMPKINS

You will need:

a variety of pumpkins in different sizes
 (the rounder varieties are better)

a paint brush

black, white and gold acrylic paint

black, orange and grey card

PVA glue

Paint your pumpkins with the black acrylic paint, leaving two eye shapes.

Paint the eyes with white acrylic paint. Once the whites of the eyes have dried, paint the pupils black. You can paint around the pupils with gold paint for the irises.

For the ears, cut out two triangles of black card. Bend back a small flap along the base of the triangle, then stick the ears on to the pumpkin by gluing down the folded flap with PVA glue.

For the nose, cut out a triangle of orange card. Cut three thin strips of grey card for the whiskers and stick them to the back of the nose. Glue this onto the face of the pumpkin. Ta da!

WEST INDIAN CURRY LAMB SHANKS
WITH FRIED PUMPKIN

Technically this should be made with goat shanks. I've used lamb shanks in this recipe because we can access them more easily, but goat shanks, if you can find them, are brilliant (I buy mine online from Cabrito). Also, to be really authentic, this recipe should be made using proper old-school blended Caribbean curry powder. I love blending my own spices and would argue that blending your own tastes that little bit better, but if you want to use ready-made West Indian curry powder, just use 2 tablespoons to replace all the spices. There isn't much that's Halloween-ish about this dish, but I think the stewiness, where the meat is actually falling off the bone, and the spiciness embrace the season, plus serving it with fried pumpkin is a nod to Halloween. Most importantly, it's just a lovely party dish that really brings people together. I am only using 6 shanks to feed 8. This isn't a misprint. I really believe that a whole shank is waaaay too much meat for one person, and when the meat falls off the bone as you serve it, the bones can just be used to garnish a big platter full of curry underneath. I've used brown rice in the rice and peas because I prefer its flavour and texture.

6 lamb or goat shanks

2 tablespoons coconut oil, plus extra for frying the pumpkin

2 large onions, finely chopped

8 garlic cloves, bashed and peeled

1–2 Scotch bonnet chillies, deseeded and chopped

2 tablespoons ground coriander

1 tablespoon ground cumin

2 teaspoons freshly ground black pepper

6 cardamom pods, crushed

4 cloves

1 teaspoons ground fenugreek

2 teaspoons ground cinnamon

2 teaspoons ground ginger

1 teaspoon ground turmeric

6 large tomatoes, roughly chopped, then blitzed to a paste

500ml (18fl oz) chicken stock

Heat the oven to 190°C/170°C fan (375°F), Gas Mark 5. Season the lamb or goat shanks with salt and pepper and brown them in the coconut oil in a large casserole pan, in small batches. You want to get a good even brown colour all over the meat. Set aside on a plate when done.

Meanwhile, bung the onions, garlic, chillies and spices into a food processor and blitz to a paste. The whole spices may not completely grind up, but that's OK. When the meat's browned, add a spot more oil to the pan and slowly fry the curry paste over a very low heat for around 5 minutes, or until it has reduced in volume and is starting to turn a little golden. Pour over the tomato paste and chicken stock, add the bay leaf, thyme and chopped coriander and give it a good stir. Add the brown sauce and the salt and stir again.

Put the shanks back into the pan and cover with a lid. Pop into the oven and cook for 3 hours, making sure to stir every so often. The stew is ready when the meat is falling off the bone and the sauce is rich and full of flavor (if you pull one of the bones it should slip out easily). Check the seasoning. If you think the sauce needs reducing to increase its flavour, remove the meat from the casserole while you reduce the liquid.

1 bay leaf

a few thyme sprigs

a good handful of fresh coriander (leaves and roots, chopped), plus extra to garnish

2 tablespoons brown sauce

1 teaspoon salt

800g pumpkin, cut into 1cm (½ inch) slices

sea salt flakes and freshly ground black pepper

For the rice & peas

400g (14oz) brown rice

¾ teaspoon salt

1 x 400g (14oz) can of coconut milk

a few thyme sprigs

1 garlic clove, smashed

2 x 400g (14oz) cans of red kidney beans

To make the rice, place all the ingredients except the beans in a pan. Fill the coconut milk can with of water and pour it into the pan, then repeat. Cover with a lid, then bring to the boil and cook for 20 minutes, or until almost all the liquid has been absorbed. Add both cans of kidney beans (drain the juice from one can, and include all the contents of the other). Cover and cook for another 10 minutes, then turn the heat off and leave it to steam for 10 minutes. The rice is ready when it's cooked all the way through, puffed up and fluffy.

When the rice is about 10 minutes away from being ready, heat some coconut oil in a frying pan. Season the pumpkin slices with salt and pepper and fry them in batches for 3–4 minutes on each side, or until they are golden brown and cooked through. I keep each batch warm in the oven under the lid of the curry while I cook the next batch – that way the pumpkin absorbs even more flavour from the curry.

If you have a mammoth platter, serve the curry and rice together, topped with the fried pumpkin and garnished with stacks of coriander. Otherwise I think it's totally fine to serve the curry in the casserole, but make sure you have place mats at the ready!

FRIED PUMPKIN & RICOTTA GNOCCHI
WITH SAGE, GORGONZOLA CREAM SAUCE & ROASTED PECANS

Pumpkin makes brilliant gnocchi. As a girl who hates making pasta, I find gnocchi truly the easiest thing to make. A great use for pumpkin purée, these little dumplings are first poached, then cooked in a sage and pecan butter to crisp up the edges at the same time as making a brilliant brown butter sauce. BUT THAT'S NOT IT! It's then served on top of a rich, creamy Gorgonzola cream sauce, making a complete seasonal dish. Two words: Game. Changer...

250g (9oz) plain flour, plus more for dusting 200g (7oz) whole-milk ricotta cheese (or you can use cottage cheese)

400g (14oz) Pumpkin Purée (see page 13)

2 large free-range egg yolks

2 teaspoons sea salt flakes, plus more as needed

2 teaspoons brown sugar

¼ teaspoon freshly grated nutmeg

freshly ground white pepper

75g (2¾oz) unsalted butter

2 teaspoons finely chopped sage leaves

50g (1¾oz) pecans, roughly chopped

juice of ½ a very juicy lemon

300ml (10fl oz) crème fraîche

100g (3½oz) Gorgonzola cheese, chopped

30g (1oz) Parmesan cheese, finely grated

freshly ground black pepper

Line a baking sheet with baking parchment and lightly dust it with flour; set aside. Bring a large pot of generously salted water to the boil over a high heat.

Place the ricotta in a blender and blitz for a few seconds until gritty, like wet crumbs, but not smooth. Add the pumpkin purée, egg yolks, salt, brown sugar and nutmeg, season with a good grinding of white pepper and stir to combine. Add the flour and mix until the dough just comes together (it will be very soft and slightly sticky, but don't overwork it or the dough will become tough and heavy), adding more flour if necessary.

Flour a work surface and turn out the dough. Pat it into a rough rectangle and cut it into 4 equal pieces. Gently roll a piece into an even rope about 2cm (¾ inch) in diameter, flouring the surface as needed. Cut the rope into 2.5cm (1 inch) pieces. Lightly flour your forefinger and your thumb, and squash the gnocchi gently into perfect rectangles. Place each on the prepared baking sheet. Repeat rolling and cutting the remaining 3 dough pieces. You will have around 32 gnocchi when done.

Line a second baking sheet with baking parchment and set aside. Add about one-third of the gnocchi to the boiling water and cook for 2–3 minutes until they float, then let them cook for about 30 seconds to 1 minute more, so they're just cooked through. (You can test this by cutting one in half – it should look the same all the way through.) Remove with a slotted spoon, blotting excess water from the bottom of the spoon with paper towels or a clean kitchen towel, and transfer to the second prepared baking

RECIPE CONTINUED OVERLEAF

FRIED PUMPKIN & RICOTTA GNOCCHIS *CONT...*

sheet. Repeat, cooking the remaining gnocchi in 2 more batches. Reserve half a mug's worth of the cooking water and set it aside.

Melt half the butter in a large frying pan over a medium-high heat until foaming. Add half the sage, half the pecans and half the gnocchi and cook, shaking the pan often, until the gnocchi are browned and a little crisp, which takes about 3 minutes. Squeeze over the lemon juice. Transfer with the slotted spoon to a bowl and keep warm. Repeat with the remaining butter, sage and gnocchi.

Put the reserved gnocchi cooking water and crème fraîche into a separate pan over a lowish heat and whisk to combine. Add the Gorgonzola and Parmesan and cook, whisking occasionally, for about 3 minutes, until slightly reduced and full of flavour. Season with salt and black pepper. Place one-quarter of the sauce on each serving plate and top with one-quarter of the gnocchi, drizzling with all the sage butter from the bowl. Serve immediately.

BRAISED VEAL
WITH MARSALA, PORCINI, LEMON & SAGE

The osso bucco cut of veal has to be one of the best stewing cuts out there. It's light meat that falls off the bone when cooked properly and leaves the marrowbone centre, oozing into the sauce, making for rich and sticky gravy. Veal gets a bad rap. I feel a responsibility to eat it as a dairy eater, as veal is a by-product of the dairy industry. If we don't eat veal, it simply gets disposed of, thrown away, with no purpose at all. Either we all give up dairy or we eat veal; simple as that! Veal is also great for you and a brilliant meat to cook. When braised, like in this dish, it becomes really melty and takes on flavour so well. While not preparing this like classic osso bucco, I've still kept it Italian, cooking it in Marsala with dried porcini mushrooms, which make a fantastic and rich stock while they cook, and finishing it with lemon and sage. I like to pull the meat off the bone and the marrow out of the bone to enrich the sauce, but it's still super-cool to serve it classically on the bone, with the marrow intact to scoop out. I'd have this with the Root Vegetable Mash on page 45, or a really cheesy polenta.

50g (1¾oz) dried porcini mushrooms

4 x 200g (7oz) osso bucco steaks, cut from the veal shin

2 tablespoons olive or rapeseed oil

12–15 baby shallots or baby onions, peeled

1 garlic bulb, cut in half widthways

2 teaspoons plain flour

400ml (14fl oz) Marsala

300ml (10fl oz) fresh chicken stock

a couple of rosemary sprigs

a few thyme sprigs

1 bay leaf

1 sage sprig, plus 10 sage leaves, finely chopped

finely grated zest and juice of 1 lemon

sea salt flakes and freshly ground black pepper

Before you start cooking, bring a kettle to the boil. Pop the dried mushrooms into a bowl and cover them with about 500ml (18fl oz) of boiling water. The mushrooms will be hydrated enough to use in 15 minutes. DO NOT THROW THE MUSHROOM STOCK OUT!

Lay the steaks on a chopping board and season with salt and pepper. Heat the oil in a large lidded casserole. Brown the steaks to a deep caramel colour all over, then remove them and set aside. Add the shallots and garlic to the pan and fry for 5 minutes. Add the flour and stir-fry for 1 minute, then pour over the Marsala, the chicken stock and 300ml (10fl oz) of the porcini mushroom stock. When pouring in the mushroom stock, be careful not to use the very last bit, as sometimes the mushrooms have grit in them that sink to the bottom of the bowl. You can now strain the mushrooms, wash them and pop them into the stew too, along with the rosemary, thyme, bay leaves and the sage sprig. Pop the lid on and braise on the hob over a low-ish heat for 2½ hours, stirring every so often and scraping away at the bottom of the pan so it doesn't stick.

RECIPE CONTINUED OVERLEAF

BRAISED VEAL WITH MARSALA, PORCINI, LEMON & SAGE *CONT...*

The meat should be literally falling off the bone and the sauce really rich and sticky.

Remove the woody herbs and add the chopped sage leaves, lemon zest and juice. This will bring a new lease of life to the dish and cut though the fat. Check the seasoning, then pull out the bones, flaking the meat a little, and scoop out all the delicious marrow from the middle of them, putting it back into the stew. Serve with Root Vegetable Mash (see page 45) or a cheesy polenta and greens (I love sprout tops!)

SPIDER WEB DEVIL'S FOOD CAKE

Whatever happened to a plain old chocolate cake? I wanted to put a simple chocolate cake back on the map, so I went out and researched American baking. I generally prefer their methods, because the cakes are lighter and hold on to more moisture due to the inclusion of buttermilk and using fewer eggs and more fat. Here I have given my own take on the American classic devil's food cake, stuffing it full of salted chocolate mousse and dousing it with real chocolate icing. It's everything you want from a chocolate cake: stacks of chocolate, moisture, lightness and sponginess, and adding the creepy, but ever-so-hypnotic spider's web swirl on top makes a devilishly good cake for Halloween.

180g (6oz) self-raising flour

200g (7oz) caster sugar

50g (1¾oz) good-quality cocoa powder

¾ teaspoon bicarbonate of soda

¼ teaspoon sea salt flakes, crushed

180g (6oz) unsalted butter, at room
temperature, cut into pieces,
plus more for the tin

120ml (4fl oz) hot, strong-brewed coffee

120ml (4fl oz) buttermilk

1 teaspoon vanilla extract

2 large free-range eggs, at room
temperature

For the mousse filling

100g (3½oz) milk chocolate

200ml (7fl oz) double cream

80g (2¾oz) unsalted butter

½ teaspoon vanilla extract

a pinch of sea salt flakes, crushed

For the chocolate glaze and web

200ml (7fl oz) double cream

100g (3½oz) milk chocolate

100g (3½oz) dark chocolate

2 tablespoons glucose (but honey
would do)

1 teaspoon vanilla extract

50g (1¾oz) white chocolate

Heat the oven to 190°C/170°C fan (375°F), Gas Mark 5.

Butter and line two 20cm (8 inch) cake tins and set aside. Sift the flour, sugar, cocoa powder, bicarbonate of soda and salt into a large mixing bowl or into the bowl of a stand mixer fitted with the paddle attachment (if in a large bowl, use electric beaters). Add the butter, then turn on your machine or beaters and blend until the butter is fully blended in and the mixture resembles breadcrumbs.

Stir the hot coffee, buttermilk and vanilla together and add it all at once to the flour mixture, blending until smooth. Break the eggs into a small dish and stir them with a fork, then add them to the batter, again blending on medium speed just until smooth. Divide the batter evenly between the prepared tins and tap them on the counter to eliminate any bubbles.

Bake the cakes for 30 minutes, or until a skewer inserted into the centre of the cake comes out clean. Cool the cakes for 20 minutes in their tins, then tip out on to a cooling rack to cool completely to room temperature. The cakes can be baked a day ahead, wrapped and stored at room temperature before filling and icing.

RECIPE CONTINUED OVERLEAF

SPIDER WEB DEVIL'S FOOD CAKE *CONT...*

For the mousse filling, place the chocolate and cream in a heatproof bowl and place it over a pan of barely simmering water. Stir the chocolate and cream occasionally and gently until all the chocolate has melted and the mixture is smooth. Remove the bowl from the heat and whisk in the butter, vanilla and salt. The mixture will become a pale and fluffy mousse. Let it cool completely to room temperature. Place the base of the cake on a wire rack set over a plate that's larger than the cake (this is to catch the chocolate glaze that falls off the edge). Spoon over the chocolate mousse and sandwich with the other cake. The mousse will make a thick layer – swipe round the edge of the cake to even out the sides, a bit like a builder would when using filler on a wall.

For the chocolate glaze, melt the cream, milk chocolate, dark chocolate and glucose together in a heatproof bowl set over a pan of barely simmering water. Melt the white chocolate in another bowl, using the same method, and pour into a small piping bag with a fine nozzle. Working quickly, pour the dark chocolate icing over the middle of the cake. With a palette knife, use long strokes to push the icing over the sides to create an even coating over the whole cake. Starting slightly off centre, pipe a white chocolate spiral from the middle of the cake out to the edges (the tighter the lines, the more dramatic the effect). Take a cocktail stick and, starting from the centre, pull it through the white chocolate to the edges. Repeat, working around the cake, to create a spider's web effect. Let the icing set for about 20–30 minutes before slicing and eating. This cake isn't one that will keep, so to enjoy it at its best be sure to eat it within a couple of days.

"BLOODY" MERINGUE BONES

While filming *Cooks to Market* many years ago, I came across a couple of talented young pastry chefs working in Hackney in London. They came on the show and developed what we now know as their meringue kisses, and the "Meringue Girls" have gone on to achieve stacks: a shop, numerous pop-up street food ventures, TV appearances and best-selling cookbooks. I could not be more proud of Stacie and Alex. Their meringue-making technique has been fine-tuned – it's a mix of Swiss and Italian meringue, made by heating the caster sugar until it's really hot (not melted like in Italian meringue) and beating it into stiff-peaked egg whites. It creates a really firm, crunchy meringue but with a marshmallowy middle. You can make white bones using this mix, but here I've folded in some freeze-dried fruit powder (I buy this online from www.souschef.co.uk), then made them look bloody by smearing the inside of a piping bag with dark-red food colouring. (See photograph on page 30.)

300g (10½oz) caster sugar

5 large free-range egg whites

1 tablespoon freeze-dried cherry or plum powder, plus extra for sprinkling

tiny amount of dark red gel food colouring

Preheat your oven to 220°C/200°C fan (425°F), Gas Mark 7 and line a baking tray with baking parchment. Pour the caster sugar on to the tray and heat it in the oven for 7 minutes. (Heating the sugar helps to create a glossy, stable mixture.)

Meanwhile, whisk the egg whites in a free-standing mixer or using an electric hand whisk in a non-plastic bowl. Whisk slowly at first, allowing small stabilizing bubbles to form, then increase the speed until the egg whites form stiff peaks.

Take the sugar out of the oven and reduce the oven temperature to 140°C/120°C fan (275°F), Gas Mark 1. With your mixer on full speed, very slowly spoon the hot sugar into the beaten egg whites, making sure the mixture comes back up to stiff peaks after each addition of sugar. Once you have added all the sugar, continue to whisk on full speed until you have a smooth, stiff and glossy mixture, then fold through the freeze-dried fruit powder.

Take 2 disposable piping bags and spoon half the meringue mixture into one of the bags, ensuring there are no air bubbles – this will be for the white bones. For the "bloody bones", turn the other piping bag inside out, and using a pastry brush and a spot of the red gel food colouring, brush three stripes of colour on to the bag. Turn the bag round the right way again and fill with the meringue mix. With sharp scissors, cut the tip of each piping bag to make a 2cm (¾ inch) hole. Line 2 baking trays with baking parchment, piping a little of the mixture into each corner first to secure the parchment in place.

Create meringue bone shapes by holding the piping bag upright and piping a heart shape, then keep the bag flowing down in a line and finish with an upside down heart. This takes a bit of practice, so don't be alarmed if you don't get it right the first time! My tip is to keep the bag higher above the tray than you think you need to. Sprinkle some of the meringues with some extra fruit powder – I like this to be a bit random, but neat freaks may want it to be more even.

Bake for 1 hour, until the bases come off the baking paper cleanly. You want them to be still mallowy in the centre. Leave them to cool before serving.

PLUM, CHERRY, CARDAMOM & PISTACHIO ETON MESS

* SERVES 6
* PREPARATION TIME: 15 MINUTES
* COOKING TIME: 20 MINUTES, PLUS COOLING

The best summer pudding is NOT summer pudding (that's the worst), but Eton Mess: strawberries, cream and meringue, all bashed together in a sticky, crunchy, creamy mess. It's the laziest pudding about, too. So here's the idea. You've made the meringue bones for a party, but now it's time to do something cool with them. Berries are out of season, but plums are in. A raw plum doesn't quite do what a cooked one does in a pudding, so we're going to make a stonking compote spiked with cardamom, then ripple it with vanilla cream and said meringue bones. Finish with freeze-dried cherries, not the raisin sort (this may sound like I've lost my mind, but they really round the pudding off and look beautiful to boot), and chopped pistachios for added crunch. As the Irish would say, it looks and tastes "DEADLY"! (See photograph on page 31.)

350g (12oz) plums

3 tablespoons caster sugar

6 cardamom pods, lightly crushed

2 tablespoons lemon juice

400ml (14fl oz) double cream

1 tablespoon icing sugar

seeds from 1 vanilla pod or 1 teaspoon vanilla extract

12 Meringue Bones (see page 32), half roughly chopped and half cut in two

2 tablespoons freeze-dried cherries, chopped

2 tablespoons pistachios, chopped

Halve and stone the plums and place them in a large pan. Add the sugar, cardamom, lemon juice and 3 tablespoons of water. Bring to a gentle simmer and cook for 15–20 minutes, until the plums are tender and swimming in a little juice. Set aside until cold, then remove the cardamom pods and mash the plums roughly with a fork. If you wanted to be really cheffy, you could blitz half the plums in a blender to a purée and mix it with the rest of the chunky ones.

Whip the cream with the icing sugar and vanilla and gently stir in the plum mixture and chopped meringue bones, giving an only-just-rippled effect. Spoon into a large trifle bowl and garnish with the chopped cherries and pistachios, with the halved meringue bones placed so that they stick out of the dish in a menacing way. Serve straight away, or the meringue goes soggy.

BAKED RICE PUDDING
WITH CARDAMOM POACHED PLUMS

I never knew anything but baked rice pudding when I was growing up. It was only as a teen that I would see vats of the stuff you can pour into a bowl. My mum insisted on baking hers. While I do like creamed rice in a can, I am dedicated to a baked version and the DELICIOUS skin it forms. Mine is improved with more liquid, so it's gooier and creamier, and I've put both bay and vanilla seeds in there for a more comforting flavour. You can eat this on its own, but I like it with cardamom poached plums.

100g (3½oz) pudding rice

300ml (10fl oz) double cream

700ml (1¼ pints) whole milk

50g (1¾oz) chopped unsalted butter

seeds of 1 vanilla pod

a very generous fresh grating of
  nutmeg

1 bay leaf

cardamom poached plums
  (see page 33), to serve

Preheat the oven to 180°C/160°C fan (350°F), Gas Mark 4.

In a 1½ litre (2¾ pint) baking dish, mix together all the ingredients. Cover with foil and bake in the oven for 45 minutes.

Remove the foil, stir and finish cooking uncovered for a further 30–45 minutes, or until a darkish skin has formed and the rice underneath is cooked and gooey and creamy. It really is as easy as that!

Remember, remember
the fifth of November
the Gunpowder treason and plot.

I see no reason,
why Gunpowder treason
Should ever be forgot.

Guy Fawkes, Guy Fawkes,
t'was his intent
To blow up King and Parliament.
Three score barrels were laid below
To prove old England's overthrow.

By God's mercy he was catch'd
With a darkened lantern
and burning match.

So, holler boys, holler boys,
Let the bells ring.
Holler boys, holler boys,
God save the King.

And what shall we do with him?
Burn him!

This traditional English nursery rhyme refers to 5th November, 1605, when Guy Fawkes, a member of the Catholic "Gunpowder Plot" group, was discovered guarding explosives planted in the Houses of Parliament in London. He was arrested with the intention of blowing it to smithereens, along with the Protestant King James I in the process. To give thanks for the apparent act of God that spared the King's life, and also to serve as a warning to anyone else with similar notions, "An Acte for a Public Thanksgiving to Almighty God Everie Yeere of the Fifte Day of November" was declared across the land. Bonfires were lit in towns and villages, with explosions and fireworks set off to represent the gunpowder, accompanied by music, food and drink.

Wherever you are in the world, finding a reason to celebrate the season outdoors with a bonfire is fun. Here in the UK, we celebrate Guy Fawkes' Night (or Bonfire Night) on 5th November. It has always carried strong anti-Establishment overtones: the tradition of "Penny for the Guy" began in the late 18th century, with children wheeling around effigies of Guy Fawkes while begging for money. The effigies would then be burnt on a bonfire after dark. These practices still exist in rural England, but you're more likely to find effigies of politicians thrown into the flames nowadays!

I can't think of eating in the winter months without thinking of sausages, so I've included recipes for a warming sausage casserole, sausage hotpot and sausage pastries, as well as recipes for apple fritters and pumpkin doughnuts to take advantage of the seasonal foods available at this harvest time of year. Even though your mitts might be freezing, don a big coat and warm your hands with a hot hand pie or a mug of hot chocolate. There is no reason why we can't feast al fresco – we're just doing it "winter style"!

Sparkle
& pop

BUTTERY ROSEMARY ROASTED CHESTNUTS

The scent of roasting chestnuts symbolizes winter food, but they remain a British street food, with few people actually roasting them at home. Now listen – buying them from a street vendor is good and all, BUT they tend to dry out and are not as good as when you roast them yourself. While it's a nice idea, we're not all able to roast them over an open fire, so a really hot oven is the next best thing, with rosemary. They are then slathered in butter, salt and nutmeg and munched with your fingers while having drinks before a meal. A fun seasonal life-changer!

1kg (2lb 4oz) fresh unshelled chestnuts

2 tablespoons olive or rapeseed oil

2–3 rosemary sprigs

2 teaspoons sea salt flakes

a good fresh grating of nutmeg

100g (3½oz) unsalted butter, melted

freshly ground black pepper

Heat the oven to 260°C/240°C fan (500°F), Gas Mark 10. That's really hot, I know. Some ovens don't go THAT hot, so if that's the case for you, just get your oven to as hot as it will go. Place a large sheet of foil on a baking dish or tray. Place the chestnuts, flat sides down, on a work surface. Using a utility knife or a sharp paring knife, carefully cut through the shell on the rounded side of each chestnut to score an "X". Put them into a bowl. Bring a kettle of water to the boil, pour it over the chestnuts, and let them soak for 1 minute (this helps them steam while roasting).

Drain the chestnuts and pat dry, then place in a mixing bowl. Add the oil, rosemary, salt, nutmeg and half the butter. Season with pepper and toss to coat thoroughly. Arrange the chestnuts in a single layer in the centre of the foil (a few might overlap), then gather up the edges of the foil around the chestnuts, leaving a large opening at the top.

Roast until the chestnut skins begin to curl up and the chestnuts are cooked through – about 35 minutes, depending on the size and age of the nuts.

Transfer the chestnuts to a platter, using a spatula to scrape in any butter and spices with them, and toss to coat. Season with more salt, if desired. Serve hot, and warn guests about burny fingers.

VENISON "OSSO BUCCO" STEW
WITH PORT, HEIRLOOM CARROTS & BACON

Here, I've used the osso bucco leg cut, which needs slooooow cooking to break down all the sinew and gelatine, making a really soft and flavourful eat, plus you get the bone marrow, too. This makes a fantastically rich sauce. It has to be served with filthy rich and buttery mash, bordering on the edge of being pomme purée.

3 tablespoons olive oil

8 osso bucco cuts of venison (get these from your butcher)

1 onion, cut into chunks

1 carrot, finely chopped

1 bay leaf

a few thyme sprigs

5 whole juniper berries

4 cloves

1 tablespoon tomato purée

1 tablespoon plain flour

300ml (10fl oz) red wine

200ml (7fl oz) port

600ml (20fl oz) beef stock

1 teaspoon redcurrant jelly

sea salt flakes and freshly ground black pepper

For the garnish

1 tablespoon unsalted butter

100g (3½oz) thick-cut, good-quality smoked bacon or pancetta, cut into thin lardons

3 large carrots (ideally orange, white and purple), peeled and cut into elegant slices

1 teaspoon finely chopped parsley leaves

Heat 2 tablespoons of olive oil in a casserole pan and brown the venison, then remove from the pan with a slotted spoon. Add the onion, carrot, herbs, juniper and cloves and fry gently for 10–15 minutes, or until softened and tinged golden. Add the tomato purée and cook for another 2–3 minutes on a higher heat so that caramelization begins in the pan. Add the flour and mix it really well into the veg. You need to let it cook with the vegetables and fat for about a minute, otherwise the stew will be cloudy and taste floury.

Pour over the red wine, port and stock, then pop the meat back into the pan, put the lid on, and put into the oven for 2½ hours, or until the meat is tender and the sauce has reduced a little, but is not too thick. Remove from the oven and leave to rest for 10 minutes with the lid on.

While the stew is resting, heat a frying pan and add the butter. Fry the bacon until the fat has rendered but the bacon is not quite golden, then add the carrots and sauté until the bacon is crisping up and the carrots are lightly caramelized. Add the parsley, remove from the heat and set aside.

OK, so here's where I go a bit barmy... What I do now is I remove the venison, VERY CAREFULLY so as not to allow the meat to break up too much. I then strain the vegetables out of the sauce, reserving the sauce and disposing of the veg. Some people find this wasteful – it's a tricky decision, because it's so much more refined when it's been strained, but if you don't want to lose the stewed veg, do keep them. The sauce will be nice and glossy after sieving, and the flavour will be almost there.

Pop the sauce back into the casserole and stir in the redcurrant jelly and seasoning, along with the meat and the bacony fried carrots. Give a good but gentle stir and put back into the oven with the lid off for another 30 minutes. When you remove it from the oven, the stew should be thick and reduced and full of flavour. Leave to rest for another 10 minutes and you are good to go!

'NDUJA SAUSAGE ROLLS

'Nduja is an Italian meat purée that's highly spiced with paprika. You can buy it from Italian delis or online, but if you can't find it you can use 300g (10½oz) of cooking chorizo, casing removed, blitzed in a food processor with 1 teaspoon of smoked paprika and 1 teaspoon of olive oil. In this recipe I've smeared the inside of the pastry with apple sauce to lift the flavours. It's grateful for the sweetness, and I've garnished with chilli flakes and a clever blend of salt, fennel and elderflower that I stumbled across – alternatively, just use ordinary sea salt flakes. The salt really makes them look super-cool and you get a spot more flavour, but it's not completely necessary. These are delicious as a hand pie but are also great with mash, onion gravy and greens as a proper dinner!

450g (1lb) good-quality outdoor-reared pork sausagemeat, or about 8 sausages, squeezed out of their skins

250g (9oz) 'nduja

100g (3½oz) Parmesan cheese, finely grated

a pinch of ground mace

plain flour, for dusting

1 x 320g (11½oz) packet of ready-rolled all-butter puff pastry

4 tablespoons apple sauce

1 large free-range egg, lightly beaten

sea salt flakes and freshly ground black pepper

For the elderflower, fennel & chilli garnish (optional)

1 tablespoon elderflower and fennel flavoured sea salt

½ tablespoon red chilli flakes

Place the sausagemeat in a mixing bowl along with the 'nduja, Parmesan, mace, salt and pepper, then really get your hands in there and squidge it all together.

Dust a work surface with flour, then lay out the pastry and roll it a little thinner, about 2mm (¹⁄₁₆ inch) thick. Cut the pastry into 3 across its width, then spread just over 1 tablespoon of apple sauce along each strip.

Divide the sausagemeat mix into 3 and form into 3 long sausages the same length as the pastry strips. Place on top of the apple sauce-covered pastry. Brush the edges of the pastry with the beaten egg, then fold it over the sausages so the meat is encased in pastry. Glaze the pastry with beaten egg, turn over and glaze the other side, then pop them into the fridge for 30 minutes.

Heat the oven to 220°C/200°C fan (425°F), Gas Mark 7.

Mix the salt blend and the chilli flakes together. Place the sausage rolls on a board and cut one either into 4 or into lots of small, bite-sized rolls. Score the tops neatly with a sharp knife, if you want. Pop them on to a baking sheet, sprinkle with some of the garnishing salt and bake for 20 minutes for the small ones or 30 minutes for the larger ones.

Remove from the oven and leave to cool for 10 minutes. Eat them warm.

SAUSAGE, TOMATO, PRESERVED LEMON, CAPER & OLIVE CASSEROLE

In Britain, we often frown upon the sausage casserole as something that is all too common. That might be, but who doesn't love a sausage recipe? It's something you learn as a food writer. The more you try to push exotic recipes, the more you actually realize the stuff you want to eat is the most conventional and comforting. It happens in almost every culture. In France they have the simple cassoulet, in Italy they braise sausages with lentils, and in Korea a favourite soup is made with blood sausage. So here I have taken influence from Italy, with a recipe inspired by my good friend and Michelin-starred (Italian) chef Angela Hartnett – sausages braised in wine and tomatoes, with other salty ingredients such as capers, olives and preserved lemons – for a casserole that sits as well on cheesy polenta as it does on pasta or cauliflower "rice".

2 tablespoons olive oil

8 sausages (I love the Italian ones with fennel)

1 onion, finely chopped

1 celery stick, thinly sliced on a slight angle

4 garlic cloves, finely chopped

a pinch of dried chilli flakes

200ml (7fl oz) white wine

2 x 400g (14oz) cans of chopped plum tomatoes

a few thyme sprigs, leaves stripped

1 bay leaf

2 preserved lemons, thinly sliced

2 tablespoons capers, drained

80g (2¾oz) good olives (I use large green Castelvetrano olives, but use whatever you like), pitted and sliced

a handful of basil leaves

sea salt flakes and freshly ground black pepper

Heat half the oil in a casserole over a medium heat. Brown the sausages all over and set aside. Reduce the heat, then add the remaining oil and fry the onion gently for 10 minutes, or until softened. Add the celery, garlic and chilli flakes and fry for a further minute. Pour over the wine and tomatoes, add the thyme and bay, then put the sausages back into the pan and leave to cook over a very low heat for 30 minutes. You are looking for the sausages to be cooked through and the sauce to begin to thicken and become rich.

Add the preserved lemons, capers, olives and basil for the last 10 minutes of cooking. When it's ready the sauce will be full of savoury umami flavour. Season with plenty of salt and pepper, and serve with really cheesy polenta, or over pasta with grated Parmesan cheese.

OLD-SCHOOL SAUSAGE HOTPOT & ROOT VEGETABLE MASH

Let me be frank here – this is a sausage casserole – but I assure you it's not just any sausage casserole. You know when you go to a really good restaurant or gastropub and order sausage and mash, and the gravy is super-sticky and tastes as rich as the gravy you get from any good roast dinner? Well, this is going to give you that rich gravy. Plus, the sausages are grateful for a braise. They suck up the flavour and stay super-moist. It's the sort of dinner you can pop into the oven, go out to see a firework display, then come back and it's cooking away happily and gently, ready for your return.

1 tablespoon vegetable oil

8 good-quality outdoor-reared pork sausages

3 onions, finely sliced

1 tablespoon plain flour

200ml (7fl oz) dry cider

500ml (18fl oz) fresh beef stock,

a rosemary sprig

a few thyme sprigs

1 teaspoon redcurrant jelly (optional)

sea salt flakes and freshly ground black pepper

For the root vegetable mash

1 small celeriac

2 carrots, peeled

1 swede

2–3 tablespoons unsalted butter

2 tablespoons milk or cream

freshly grated nutmeg

Heat the oven to 220°C/200°C fan (425°F), Gas Mark 7. Heat the oil in a casserole pan and fry the sausages until they are browned, but not cooked through, then remove and set aside. Add the onions and fry slowly for 15 minutes, or until they have fully softened and started to go golden. Stir in the flour and cook for 10 minutes. Pour over the cider, bring to the boil and cook for 2 minutes. Add the stock and herbs, put the lid on, and pop into the oven for 35 minutes, or until it is bubbling, thickened and full of flavour. If using, stir through the redcurrant jelly just before serving. Taste and adjust the seasoning.

Meanwhile, to make the mash, chop all the veggies into small cubes and put them into a pan of cold water with some salt. Bring to the boil, then boil gently for 20 minutes or until completely cooked through. Drain, then allow the vegetables to steam in the colander for 5 minutes. Mash with a potato masher or ricer, then add the butter, milk or cream, a grating of nutmeg and seasoning and beat furiously until it comes together into a smooth mash. It won't be quite the same texture as mashed potatoes as these veggies are not as starchy. Serve alongside the sausages.

* MAKES 6
* PREPARATION TIME: 15 MINUTES,
  PLUS CHILLING
* COOKING TIME: 30 MINUTES

CHEDDAR, ONION & POTATO HAND PIE

A classic Cheddar, onion and potato pie is made just with those ingredients, but I've always found it to be too dry, so I've added my own twist and made this with a rich Cheddar cheese sauce that oozes a little when served straight from the oven. It's in keeping with the hand pie idea, so not only will it warm you from within, it will keep your mitts warm, too.

1 tablespoon olive oil

1 tablespoon unsalted butter

2 large onions, peeled and thinly sliced

1 large baking potato, peeled and very thinly sliced

300ml (10fl oz) milk

10g (¼oz) plain flour, plus extra for dusting

200g (7oz) Cheddar cheese, grated

1 teaspoon English mustard

a pinch of freshly grated nutmeg

a few thyme leaves

1 x 320g (11oz) packet of ready-rolled all-butter puff pastry

1 free-range egg, beaten

sea salt flakes and freshly ground black pepper

Heat the olive oil and butter in a small(ish) pan over a low heat, then throw in the onions and fry for 20 minutes, or until they are soft, sweet and golden. Set aside to cool for 10 minutes.

Meanwhile, put the potatoes into a pan with the milk and bring to the boil, then turn off the heat. Leave for 2 minutes, then strain out the milk, reserving it for the sauce.

Mix the flour into the onions and cook gently over a low heat for 1 minute, then take off the heat and slowly whisk in the milk. Put back on the heat and continue to whisk until the sauce comes to the boil, then cook for 1 minute, until it has thickened. Add the cheese, mustard, nutmeg, thyme and seasoning, and cook just until the cheese has melted. The sauce will be quite thick. Stir the sauce into the potatoes and leave to cool for 1 hour, then place in the fridge for another hour. The filling has to be used cold.

On a floured surface, roll the pastry out about 2mm (¹⁄₁₆ inch) thick, and cut out 6 rectangles. Divide the filling between the rectangles, making sure you place it right in the centre. Brush the edges of the pastry with some of the beaten egg, then fold over and crimp the edges. Add some star shapes using the pastry trimmings, if you like. Lay the pies on a floured baking sheet and brush them with the rest of the beaten egg. Transfer to the fridge and chill for 15 minutes.

Heat the oven to 210°C/190°C fan (410°F), Gas Mark 6½.

Brush each pie again generously with egg, then bake for 30 minutes until golden and the filling is bubbling and gooey. Best served warm, with a crisp green salad.

PUMPKIN & SWEET POTATO DOUGHNUTS

This recipe is from my friend Martin Morales, the chef and restaurateur of the Ceviche restaurants in London. The real name of these doughnuts is *picarones*, and they're made from sweated-down sweet potato and pumpkin that is made into a dough in a similar way to gnocchi, but leavened with yeast. They are then deep-fried and plunged into a bath of the sweetest, stickiest and spiciest glaze, which soaks into the outer layer, making a brilliantly flavourful and chewy crust. They are fantastic in winter and there is something so seasonal about making them for Halloween, Bonfire Night or Thanksgiving.

5cm cinnamon stick

4 cloves

1 tablespoon green aniseeds or 1 star anise

4 tablespoons caster sugar

200g (7oz) pumpkin (peeled weight), peeled, deseeded and chopped into chunks

200g (7oz) sweet potato (peeled weight), peeled and chopped into chunks

20g (¾oz) fresh yeast (or 1 teaspoon dried instant yeast)

2 tablespoons warm water

½ teaspoon sea salt flakes

250g (9oz) plain flour (you may need to up this to 300g/10½oz if you find the dough is very wet), plus extra for dusting

vegetable oil, for deep-frying

Tie the spices in a small square of muslin (the aniseed will be difficult to remove otherwise), and put it into a saucepan along with 2 tablespoons of the sugar, the chopped pumpkin and sweet potato. Cover with cold water, bring to the boil and simmer until the pumpkin and sweet potato are soft. Drain thoroughly (you want it as dry as possible) and remove the spice bag. Blitz the pumpkin and sweet potato in a food processor until you have a smooth purée.

Meanwhile, dissolve the yeast in the warm water along with the remaining sugar. Leave in a warm place for 15 minutes, until the mixture has started to develop a foamy surface.

Add the salt and flour to the purée, then add the yeast mixture. Beat together until you have a smooth dough. The dough is meant to be sticky, but you need to be able to handle it enough to form rings, so add more flour 20g (¾oz) at a time if you find it very wet. Cover the bowl with a clean, damp tea towel and leave to rest in a warm place for 1 hour, or until it has doubled in size.

While the dough is proving, make the syrup. Put all the syrup ingredients into a saucepan and add just enough water to cover. Bring to the boil and simmer until it has reduced to a thick syrup. Leave until cool – the flavours will continue to infuse. Strain into a shallow bowl.

To form the doughnuts, first tip out the dough on to a floured surface. Then, with floured hands, form it into an oblong, about 12 x 5cm (4½ x 2 inches). Using a sharp knife, cut the dough into 10–12 sections. Roll each piece a little to lengthen, then quickly shape into a ring by binding the ends together.

For the syrup

200g (7oz) dark soft brown sugar

1 cinnamon stick

1 star anise

6 cloves

pared zest of 1 orange

1 pineapple, skin only

½ teaspoon sea salt flakes

You will need to work quickly, as it's quite tricky and messy to handle, but remember, part of the charm of these doughnuts is their rustic appearance!

If you have a deep-fat fryer, heat the oil to 180°C (350°F). If not, pour oil into a large, deep saucepan to a depth of about 5cm (2 inches), making sure it is no more than half full. To test if the oil is hot enough, drop in a nugget of dough – if it sizzles and turns golden, the oil is ready.

Fry the doughnuts in small batches in the hot oil. They will grow slightly in size and float to the surface. Flip the doughnuts over once during the frying process – they should look dark golden brown and crisp when cooked.

Remove the doughnuts from the oil and drain on kitchen paper. Dunk them into the syrup and flip them around until they are covered in the sauce so as to glaze them. Whip them out and pop them on to a serving plate. Serve warm, on their own or with vanilla ice cream.

APPLE CIDER
FRITTERS

Apple fritters straight out of the fryer, tossed into a spiced sugar and eaten hot out of napkins while watching the fireworks, are the stuff of memories for me. Somewhere between a doughnut and a fritter, they symbolize everything that's wonderful about the winter season. They are AMAZING with vanilla or salted caramel ice cream.

150g (5½oz) self-raising flour

30g (1oz) cornflour

½ teaspoon baking powder

2 free-range eggs, beaten

150ml (¼ pint) cold cider
   or fizzy water

4 small British Braeburn apples

vegetable oil, for deep frying

100g (3½oz) caster sugar

1 teaspoon mixed spice

½ teaspoon ground cinnamon

½ teaspoon sea salt flakes

vanilla or salted caramel ice cream,
   to serve

Place the flours and baking powder in a mixing bowl. Make a well in the centre, then pour in the eggs and the cold cider or fizzy water. Quickly whisk together, then leave to rest for 30 minutes in the fridge. Cold batter will make extra crispy fritters.

Core the apples, then slice the tops and bottoms off them to make them into neat barrels. Cut each apple horizontally into 4 slices.

If you have a deep-fat fryer, heat the oil to 180°C (350°F). If not, pour oil into a large, deep saucepan to a depth of about 5cm (2 inches), making sure it is no more than half full. Plunge the apple slices into the batter, then deep-fry them for 2–3 minutes, or until crisp and golden and the apples are cooked through. Scoop out with a slotted spoon and drain on kitchen paper.

Mix together the caster sugar, spices and salt. While the apples are still hot, toss them into the sugar and serve straight away.

EPIC MALTED
HOT CHOCOLATE

Hot chocolate is simply sweetened cocoa and milk, but we can do better than that. If you want a hot chocolate of epic proportions you need to make it with cocoa powder and real chocolate, whole milk and malt powder, and flavour it with vanilla, clementine zest and cinnamon. It's imperative to have melty marshmallows bobbing around in the cup, with a further grating of real chocolate. We're not messing about here – you wait and see how good this tastes. You can bung a shot of brandy or whisky in there too if you want to make it illegal!

2 tablespoons malted milk drinking powder (I use Horlicks)

1 tablespoon cocoa powder

5 tablespoons milk or dark chocolate (depending on how rich you like it – I'm a child, so I go for milk), grated, or cooking buttons

½ teaspoon cornflour

a pinch of sea salt flakes

a pinch of ground cinnamon

½ teaspoon seeded vanilla extract

1 teaspoon finely grated clementine zest (about 2 clementines' worth)

600ml (20fl oz) whole milk

To serve

mini marshmallows

more grated chocolate

Melt everything together in a small pan, whisking with a small sauce whisk if you have one, or a wooden spoon if not, until it starts to thicken. Once heated to boiling point it will thicken slightly from the cornflour. Pour into 2 mugs, and top with as many marshmallows as will fit, plus more grated chocolate. Serve immediately.

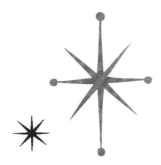

There is a wonderful array of produce available in November and December and there's no better way to celebrate than feasting with family and friends. Thanksgiving celebrations originate from when the first European settlers arrived in North America, namely Plymouth in Massachusetts, on the infamous ship the Mayflower in 1620. The first brutal winter they experienced killed almost half the community. It wasn't until they formed an alliance with the native Wampanoag tribe, who taught them to farm corn, fish, collect sap from maple trees and avoid poisonous plants, that they finally were able to sustain themselves. By the winter of 1621 they had gathered enough harvest to hold a celebratory feast, to which they invited members of the Wampanoag tribe. The chief arrived bearing five deer as a gift, so venison would almost have certainly featured on the menu. Goose, lobster, and perhaps even seal were also probable additions. Historians believe it is likely the food would have been influenced by the cooking and spicing of the Native Americans. Sugar was scarce however, so it is unlikely there would have been any cakes or pies like there are today.

After the original Pilgrim meal, despite celebrations being common in many parts of New England subsequently, it was only in 1789 that George Washington issued the very first Thanksgiving proclamation, to celebrate the end of America's War of Independence and the enactment of the Constitution. This was observed, but the date varied from state to state. It was American writer and editor Sarah Josepha Hale, (author of the famous *Mary Had a Little Lamb,* no less!), who passionately petitioned, for 36 years, for the establishment of a national holiday of Thanksgiving, in the belief that it would unite a country dangerously close to civil war. Finally in 1863 Abraham Lincoln granted her wish when he entreated Americans as God would to "commend to His tender care all those who have become widows, orphans, mourners or sufferers in the lamentable civil strife", and cementing the date as the final Thursday of November.

Like many modern interpretations of celebratory traditions, Thanksgiving has lost much of its religious or historical significance for the majority of Americans. It is most commonly viewed as an opportunity to focus on family and enjoy the bounty of the seasonal harvest. Parades and football games became central to the festivities during the early 20th century.

Now, for the food! Turkey only became ubiquitous after the mid-1800s, but now this is the centrepiece for nearly all Thanksgiving dinners. As I am English, I have put both my turkey recipes in the Christmas chapter of this book, but if you're going to celebrate Thanksgiving then you HAVE to have turkey. And potatoes, pumpkin pie, cranberry sauce and sweetcorn all feature, due to their American origins. I've incorporated all the references and influences into a modern Thanksgiving menu that celebrates seasonal ingredients and brings family and friends together.

As Brits, we celebrate Harvest Festival, so while I've looked at American recipes and New England-style foods (note the New England Clambake on page 72 which is a dreamboat of a recipe), I've taken my favourite British seasonal harvest produce and given it an American facelift.

Celebrating
the harvest

BAKED JERUSALEM ARTICHOKE, SPINACH & PARMESAN DIP

This is one of the best things I've ever made. It's really simple, too. It's classically made with globe artichokes, but here I've used more seasonal Jerusalem artichokes. Unlike the chunkier dips you find at American steakhouses, I've blended it into much more of a purée consistency. Serve it with pink and white chicory leaves and crusty bread, for dipping.

olive oil

knob of unsalted butter

250g (9oz) spinach leaves, washed

300g (10½oz) Jerusalem artichokes

400ml (14fl oz) double cream

100g (3½oz) Parmesan cheese, finely grated, plus more for topping

2 garlic cloves, grated

¼ teaspoon cayenne pepper

¼ teaspoon freshly grated nutmeg

2 free-range egg yolks

chicory leaves, separated, to serve

sea salt flakes and freshly ground black pepper

Heat the oven to 220°C/200°C fan (425°F), Gas Mark 7. Heat the oil and butter in a large pan over a medium heat, add the spinach leaves and stir until they wilt. Drain, then squeeze out any excess water with kitchen paper.

Peel the artichokes and put them into a pan of cold water. Bring to the boil, then cook for about 15 minutes, until really soft. Drain, then blend in a food processor, adding the rest of the ingredients one by one, the egg yolks last. It may look a little gritty at this point, but fear not – the baking process will sort that out. Season to taste.

Spoon the mixture into 1 or 2 ovenproof dishes (I think this looks better and stays warmer in 2 smaller dishes), smoothing the top with a knife. Cover with enough grated Parmesan to blanket the top. Bake in the oven for 20–25 minutes, during which time everything melts together and it soufflés ever so slightly and gets a brilliant crusty top with garlicky, spinachy goo underneath. Serve piping hot with chicory leaves for dipping. This is a tongue scorcher!

SERVES 6
PREPARATION TIME: 10 MINUTES
COOKING TIME: 20 MINUTES

BROWN SHRIMP GRATIN

I only ever really see brown shrimps as potted shrimps, or in brown butter with fish or maybe the odd leek, sometimes in a salad but rarely. I love the little critters. OK, so here's what I'm thinking: classic potted shrimps crossed with the brilliant ***gambas pil pil*** and gratinated. I think I may have invented the best new starter EVER.

250g (9oz) unsalted butter

2 garlic cloves, finely grated or chopped

¼–½ teaspoon chilli flakes

2 tablespoons finely chopped flat-leaf parsley

finely grated zest and juice of ½ lemon

400g (14oz) cooked brown shrimps, peeled

80g (2¾oz) white or sourdough breadcrumbs

30g (1oz) Parmesan cheese, finely grated

sea salt flakes and freshly ground black pepper

Preheat the oven to 240°C/220°C fan (475°F), Gas Mark 9.

Melt the butter in a saucepan and pour it into a clear jug. You want to use the clear butter and leave behind the milk solids, so let it settle for about 5 minutes. Pour the clarified butter into another saucepan, add the garlic and chilli and fry gently for 1–2 minutes. Take off the heat and add the parsley, lemon zest and juice and plenty of seasoning.

Divide the brown shrimps between 6 shallow ramekins and pour the garlicky butter evenly over them.

Mix together the breadcrumbs and Parmesan and divide this topping between the ramekins. Place on a baking tray and bake for 10–15 minutes, or until the crumbs start to brown and the butter is bubbling. Serve hot, with good-quality sourdough bread to plunge. It will be extra hot, so warn your guests.

SHREDDED SPROUT SALAD THREE WAYS

Ah, the shredded sprout salad. What a revelation. Brussels sprouts are so delicious eaten raw, having spent a bit of time macerating in a dressing. The dressing breaks them down and takes away the cabbageyness and they're rounded off into a superb salad leaf. I've created three different and very easy salads that really make the most of these vegetables, and are a refreshing breath of fresh air in a season of richness, when you're craving crunch. Salad one, with Parmesan, lemon and roasted almonds, is simplicity personified. Salad two, with pomegranate, pistachio, herbs and sumac, takes a Middle Eastern twist. Finally, salad three is a classic Waldorf but using sprouts as the leaf. They can all be eaten on their own, or with a main course. Shred your sprouts and eat them raw. You won't look back.

SHREDDING SPROUTS

This means that your sprouts need to be very thinly sliced. You can either do this by hand using a knife, or whizz them through the shredder/ slicer attachment of your food processor. Don't do as I did and try to cut them using a mandolin slicer or you'll risk tearing your knuckles!

SHREDDED SPROUT SALAD
WITH PARMESAN, LEMON & ROASTED ALMONDS

SERVES 4

Place 300g (10½oz) shredded sprouts in a serving bowl and toss with 3 tablespoons freshly squeezed lemon juice, 6 tablespoons olive oil and plenty of seasoning. Leave the sprouts to macerate for 15 minutes, then top with 30g (1oz) finely grated Parmesan and 100g (3½oz) roasted Marcona almonds, and serve.

SHREDDED SPROUT SALAD
WITH POMEGRANATE, PISTACHIO, HERBS & SUMAC

SERVES 4

Place 300g (10½oz) shredded sprouts in a serving bowl and toss with 2 tablespoons freshly squeezed lemon juice, 2 tablespoons pomegranate molasses, 6 tablespoons olive oil and plenty of seasoning. Leave the sprouts to macerate for 15 minutes, then sprinkle over the seeds of 1 pomegranate, 100g (3½oz) chopped pistachios, 1 tablespoon chopped dill, 1 tablespoon chopped mint leaves and 1 teaspoon sumac, and serve.

SHREDDED SPROUT WALDORF SALAD

SERVES 4

In a serving bowl, mix together 1 teaspoon Dijon mustard with 2 tablespoons freshly squeezed lemon juice, 3 tablespoons natural yoghurt, 3 tablespoons olive oil and plenty of seasoning. Add 300g (10½oz) shredded sprouts to the bowl. Leave to macerate for 15 minutes, then add 100g (3½oz) halved seedless grapes, 1 sliced eating apple, 60g (2¼oz) walnut halves and a few freshly chopped tarragon sprigs, and serve.

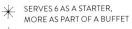
BUFFALO CAULIFLOWER
WITH BLUE CHEESE, CELERY & CUCUMBER

I tried this dish for the first time when I was last in Los Angeles. I saw it on the menu and scoffed a bit, but was kind of intrigued. I've written before about how I have a disdain for vegetarian versions of meat dishes, but this really works. It's a brilliant starter, or can be eaten as a warm salad for lunch. Surprisingly I've never written a recipe for buffalo sauce, so I quizzed all my chef friends. I've come up with a dish that's somewhere between the recipe by chef Neil Rankin, and Matt from BBQ Labs – the chicken wing aficionado of the London street food scene (and it's blooming brilliant on roasted wings, too). This is a fantastic starter, and great as part of a buffet.

100g (3½oz) rice flour

100ml (3½fl oz) water

1 teaspoon garlic powder

1 teaspoon sea salt flakes

1 head of cauliflower, chopped into bite-size florets

3 tablespoons olive oil

For the buffalo sauce

1 x 148ml (¼ pint) bottle of hot sauce (I use Frank's RedHot sauce)

150g (5½oz) unsalted butter

3 tablespoons cider vinegar

1 tablespoon Worcestershire sauce

For the blue cheese dressing

100g (3½oz) blue cheese (I like Gorgonzola)

200g (7oz) soured cream

juice of 1 lemon

lots of freshly ground black pepper

pinch of sea salt flakes

For the salad

80g (2¾oz) blue cheese

1 stick of celery, thinly sliced, plus a handful of celery leaves, torn

⅛ cucumber, halved, deseeded and thinly sliced

Preheat the oven to 240°C/220°C fan (475°F), Gas Mark 9.

Spoon the olive oil on to a non-stick baking tray and set aside. In a small bowl, mix together the rice flour, water, garlic powder and salt to make a smooth batter. Toss the cauliflower florets in the batter until evenly coated, then place on the oiled baking tray. Roast for about 12 minutes, or until the batter is crunchy and golden, then flip with a spatula and bake for another 5 minutes.

To make the sauce, put the hot sauce, butter, vinegar and Worcestershire sauce into a small pan and melt together over a medium heat. Dress the cauliflower with half the sauce and continue to roast for another 8–10 minutes, or until the cauliflower is crispy and the sauce has absorbed and is bordering on looking caramelized.

Meanwhile make the blue cheese dressing by blending together the blue cheese, soured cream, lemon, pepper and salt. Spread the dressing on a serving platter. When the cauliflower is ready it will be fiery in colour and tinged with golden brown. Toss into the rest of the buffalo sauce and add to the platter on top of the dressing. Top with the crumbled blue cheese, celery, celery leaves and cucumber.

CREAMED CORN
TWO WAYS

I like my creamed corn really creamy. Almost more like polenta. I made this for the first time with fresh corn and was amazed at how well the corn thickened up with its natural starch. For me the best texture is when half the corn is puréed and half is left chunky, and right at the end it's thinned down and flavoured with mascarpone, butter and Parmesan cheese – somewhere between classic creamed corn, polenta or its American cousin, grits. Here's my basic recipe and two ways to serve it.

8 sweetcorn cobs, stripped of their kernels

400ml (14fl oz) fresh chicken or vegetable stock

150g (5½oz) mascarpone

50g (1¾oz) Parmesan cheese, finely grated

20g (¾oz) unsalted butter

a good fresh grating of nutmeg

sea salt flakes and freshly ground black pepper

Place the corn kernels in a medium pan and pour over the stock. Bring to the boil, then reduce the heat to a low simmer. Cook for 8 minutes, then with a slotted spoon scoop out half the cooked kernels and set aside. Pour the remaining kernels and their cooking liquor into a food processor and blitz until smooth. Pour back into the saucepan and add the rest of the kernels. Cook over a medium heat for another 5 minutes. The puréed corn will start to get really thick. Stir in the mascarpone, Parmesan, butter, nutmeg and seasoning and continue to cook for another couple of minutes.

Serving suggestions

CREAMED CORN
WITH JALAPEÑO & SMOKED BACON

Cut 10 rashers of smoked streaky bacon into lardons, then fry until crisp and golden. Add slices of pickled jalapeño chilli to the pan at the last minute. Serve your creamed corn in a serving dish, topped with the crispy bacon and jalapeño mixture.

CREAMED CORN GRATIN

Pour the cooked creamed corn into a 1.5 litre (2¾ pint) gratin dish, top with a generous handful of Parmesan cheese and bake in a preheated oven at 220°C/200°C fan (400°F), Gas Mark 6 for 15 minutes, or until the cheese has melted and turned golden.

KALE, CHILLI, ANCHOVY & LEMON PESTO

I can't believe I haven't published this recipe before. It's one of my mum's, and I pretty much grew up on it as one of our favourite, more swanky ways to eat pasta. This was waaaay before kale and cavolo nero had a publicist, so they were much harder to find. This dish reeks of garlic, has a heavy backbone of umami from the anchovy, stings with chilli and all comes together with the zestiness of lemon. Slathered over any pasta, it does as good a job as, if not better than, any great basil pesto recipe, but this one is for the superfood generation.

360g (12½oz) spaghetti or linguine (I actually prefer this made with wholemeal pasta)

1 large (about 250g/9oz) bunch of cavolo nero or kale, leaves stripped from the stalks

200ml (7fl oz) olive oil

6 garlic cloves, finely chopped

1–2 red chillies, finely chopped

8–12 salted anchovies in oil

juice of ½ lemon

finely grated Parmesan cheese, to serve

sea salt flakes and freshly ground black pepper

Bring a large pan of salted water to the boil. Pop your pasta in and cook for 8–9 minutes, or until al dente. Place a sieve into the same pan of boiling water the pasta is cooking in. Plunge the cavolo nero or kale into the submerged sieve and cook for 1–2 minutes. When done, lift the sieve out; this will drain it at the same time.

Meanwhile, heat the oil in a medium to large pan. Add the garlic and chillies and cook over a low heat for a couple of minutes, or until the room is full of those great magical garlicky smells and the garlic has softened. You don't want to colour the garlic, as it will start to taste bitter. Add the anchovies and stir them until they have melted into the oil. Next add the blanched leaves and stir-fry them for a minute until they are coated in all the garlicky oil.

Transfer all this into a blender with 1 tablespoon of the pasta cooking water, the lemon juice and plenty of seasoning, and blitz until it forms a smooth paste. Drain the pasta and tip it back into the pan, then stir in the pesto and serve with stacks of freshly grated Parmesan cheese.

NEW ENGLAND CLAMBAKE

It's not massively Thanksgiving-y, but my friends on the East Coast celebrate with a clambake as well as a turkey dinner on Thanksgiving weekend. It makes perfect sense. The shellfish are bang in season, as are the corn and potatoes. I went to my friend and neighbour, Brad McDonald the chef and owner of the Lockhart and Shotgun (two of the coolest, most authentic AND delicious American restaurants in London), for his advice on how make the bouillon. We debated the strengths of Old Bay seasoning versus Zatarain's (I chose Old Bay because it's easier to get hold of and arguably more classic); whether to include prawns or not (not); which potatoes (red-skinned are the most classic, but in the UK they may be tricky to find, so any good waxy variety is super); and if it is acceptable for me to put my twist on it and French it up a bit (absolutely). The result is a slightly more polished, even more tasty, but still the same hearty version of the New England classic. Lay it out on a table lined with plenty of waxed paper and eat entirely with your fingers, plunging into the butter and hot sauce as you go. I tell you one thing, licking off the garlic-buttery, hot sauce and seafood juices dripping down your elbow is one of the world's greatest pleasures.

For the court-bouillon

2 litres (3½ pints) cold water

400ml (14fl oz) dry white wine

1 garlic bulb

1 onion, sliced

2 carrots, roughly chopped

2 sticks of celery with leaves, sliced

1 lemon, sliced

2 bay leaves

a good few thyme sprigs

a good few parsley sprigs

2½ tablespoons Old Bay seasoning

1 tablespoon sea salt flakes

600g (1lb 5oz) small red-skinned potatoes, or small waxy ones like new potatoes, halved

1 smoked Morteau sausage (or 3 smoked Andouille sausages)

2 sweetcorn cobs, cut into quarters

2 live medium lobsters

1kg (2lb 4oz) palourde clams

In a ginormous stockpot over a medium-high heat, bring the water, wine, garlic, onion, carrots, celery, lemon and herbs to the boil. Reduce the heat and simmer for 20 minutes. The aromatics will infuse into the wine and water and make a really delicious court-bouillon stock. Sieve out the veg, reserving the liquor. Clean out the stockpot, then pour the liquor back in and add the Old Bay seasoning and salt. Add the potatoes, whole sausage(s) and sweetcorn to the pot, cover, and simmer for 10 minutes. Increase the temperature and ensure the liquor is boiling, then nestle the live lobsters on top of the potatoes and sweetcorn, cover immediately with a lid and cook for 10 more minutes. Add the clams and continue to cook, covered, for 3–5 minutes more. Check to see if the clam shells have opened; if not, continue to cook until they have. Discard any clams that don't open.

Meanwhile, place all the garlic butter ingredients in a blender and blitz until you have a bright green butter. You can store this in the fridge for up to a week, and it goes with seafood and grilled steaks, but for this recipe we want it melted and the garlic cooked a little, so pop it on the hob in a small pan and melt it slowly, then cook for 1 minute or until the garlic is not quite so "raw".

For the garlic butter

4–5 garlic cloves, crushed

200g (7oz) unsalted butter

½ teaspoon Old Bay seasoning

¼ teaspoon smoked sea salt

2 generous handfuls of flat-leaf
   parsley, chopped

a squeeze of lemon juice

To serve

6 lemons, cut into wedges

Louisiana hot sauce (I use Frank's
   RedHot sauce)

crusty bread and butter

green salad

When the lobster has turned red and is cooked, carefully remove the pot from the heat and drain off and discard the cooking liquid. Take out the lobsters and the sausage. Separate the lobster claws from the bodies. Cut the bodies in half and set aside. Remove the potatoes and sausage and slice into rounds. Arrange the potatoes, sausage slices, sweetcorn, lobster and clams on a table lined with greaseproof or waxed paper, or transfer to a large platter. Pour over the garlic butter, scatter over the lemon wedges, and allow everyone to tuck in, with Louisiana hot sauce, bread and a green salad for company. (You may wish to set out some small buckets or dishes so folks know where to toss the spent lobster and clamshells.) Oh... and have plenty of napkins at the ready.

- SERVES 10–12
- PREPARATION TIME: 1 HOUR, PLUS COOLING
- COOKING TIME: 30 MINUTES FOR THE PASTRY; 1 HOUR FOR THE PIE

BROWN BUTTER
SALTED MAPLE
PUMPKIN PIE

For Brits, pumpkin pie sounds a bit on the "weirdy-woos" side, but in America, pumpkin pie is as standard as apple pie is to us. Pretty much every American household will have it for Thanksgiving. Nigella Lawson posted about a pie company on Instagram called Four & Twenty Blackbirds and I've been obsessed with their pies ever since. They do a brown butter pumpkin pie that I've adapted to make it my own with the addition of salted maple. I also enlisted the help of my American baking mate, Claire Ptak (owner of Violet Cakes in London) who advised me on how to get that perfect, wibbly centre. It needs to be a bit like a cheesecake and undercooked in the middle, as the filling will continue cooking out of the oven, but still with souffléd and puffed-up sides. This is strictly to be served with softly whipped cream. "It's sacrilege otherwise," says my American publisher, Stephanie.

For the pastry

225g (8oz) plain flour, plus extra for dusting

1 tablespoon caster sugar

a pinch of sea salt flakes

150g (5½oz) unsalted butter, chopped, plus extra for buttering the dish

1 free-range egg yolk

1 teaspoon iced water

1 teaspoon cider vinegar

To make the pastry, mix the flour, sugar and salt together in a food processor. Add the butter pieces and blend until it resembles breadcrumbs. Combine the egg yolk with the water and cider vinegar and add it to the processor, then blend until it just forms a ball of dough. Squeeze and pinch with your fingertips to bring the dough together. If the mix is too dry to bring together, add more water a teaspoon at a time. Shape it into a flat disc, wrap in clingfilm, and refrigerate for at least 1 hour, preferably overnight, to give the pastry time to relax.

Preheat the oven to 200°C/180°C fan (400°F), Gas Mark 6. Roll the pastry out on a floured surface and line a buttered 23cm (9 inch) diameter pie dish with it. The pastry will shrink when cooked, so make sure there is enough overhanging the edge of the dish. Trim neatly, then crimp the edges. Prick the base all over with a fork, line with baking parchment and fill with baking beans, then blind bake for 15 minutes, until light golden brown. Reduce the temperature to 180°C/160°C fan (350°F), Gas Mark 4, remove the baking parchment and beans and bake the pastry for a further 5 minutes to dry out.

INGREDIENTS AND RECIPE CONTINUED OVERLEAF

For the pumpkin filling

150g (5½oz) unsalted butter

125g (4½oz) brown sugar

3 tablespoons water

150ml (¼ pint) double cream

¾ teaspoon seeded vanilla extract

¾ teaspoon sea salt flakes

2 large free-range eggs (I use Burford
  browns for the orange yolks)

3 large free-range egg yolks

300g (10½oz) Pumpkin Purée
  (see page 13)

¾ teaspoon ground allspice

¾ teaspoon ground cinnamon

½ teaspoon ground ginger

a pinch of ground cloves

1 tablespoon black treacle

45ml (3 tablespoons) lemon juice

150ml (¼ pint) maple syrup

125ml (4fl oz) whole milk

75ml (2½fl oz) carrot juice

To serve

whipped cream

To make the filling, melt the butter over a medium-low heat. Continue to cook, whisking occasionally – the butter will foam and begin to turn golden, then nut brown. When the butter is nut brown, immediately add the brown sugar, whisk, and then carefully add the water to loosen. Bring the mixture to a boil and continue simmering until a sugar thermometer reads 120°C/248°F. (If you don't have a thermometer, cook until the mixture smells caramelized and starts to darken.) Whisk in the cream (the mixture will bubble rapidly) and keep whisking until smooth. Allow to cool for at least 10 minutes. Stir in the vanilla extract and salt.

Meanwhile, heat the oven again to 180°C/160°C fan (350°F), Gas Mark 4, and position the oven shelf in the centre. In a separate bowl, lightly whisk the eggs and yolks and set aside.

In the bowl of a food processor, blend the pumpkin purée with the allspice, cinnamon, ginger, cloves, treacle and lemon juice until smooth. With the machine running on low, pour the brown-butter butterscotch in a slow steady stream through the food processor's feed tube and process until combined. Stream in the egg mixture, followed by the maple syrup, milk and carrot juice, and continue blending until smooth, scraping down the sides if need be.

Pour into the pre-baked pastry case. Place the dish on a rimmed baking tray and bake for 55 minutes to 1 hour 10 minutes. The pie is ready when the edges are set and puffed slightly and the centre is no longer liquid but still quite wobbly. Allow to cool completely on a wire rack, for at least 2–3 hours. Serve slightly warm or at room temperature with softly whipped cream.

BLUEBERRY & SPELT COBBLER

I'd never tried a cobbler before making this – what a twerp – they're great! The cobbler bit is basically a scone that puffs up in the oven and soaks up the flavour from the fruit underneath. I use spelt flour in my recipe because I love the taste – it's more wholesome, but it acts similarly to plain flour and is brilliant in baking. There's something about the scone top with the oozy fruity bottom that makes an afternoon tea into a terrific pudding, especially when served with clotted cream ice cream.

For the filling

80g (2¾oz) caster sugar

1 tablespoon cornflour

a small pinch of ground cinnamon

a small pinch of sea salt flakes

600g (1lb 5oz) blueberries

finely grated zest of 1 lemon

3 tablespoons lemon juice

For the topping

120g (4¾oz) spelt flour

50g (1¾oz) caster sugar

2 tablespoons maize flour

2 teaspoons baking powder

¼ teaspoon bicarbonate of soda

¼ teaspoon sea salt flakes

100ml (3½fl oz) buttermilk

4 tablespoons unsalted butter, melted

½ teaspoon vanilla extract

For the cinnamon crunch sugar

2 teaspoons demerara or granulated sugar

¼ teaspoon ground cinnamon

To serve

clotted cream ice cream if you can find it, otherwise vanilla

Heat the oven to 200°C/180°C fan (400°F), Gas Mark 6. Mix the sugar, cornflour, cinnamon and salt together in a large bowl. Add the blueberries and mix gently until evenly coated, then add the lemon zest and juice and mix to combine. Transfer the berry mixture to a 23cm (9 inch) deep-dish pie dish. Place the dish on a baking sheet and bake for 25 minutes, or until the filling is hot and bubbling around the edges.

Meanwhile you can crack on with the topping: whisk the flour, sugar, maize flour, baking powder, bicarbonate of soda and salt together in a large bowl. Whisk the buttermilk, melted butter and vanilla together in a small bowl. A minute before the blueberries come out of the oven, add the wet ingredients to the dry ingredients and stir until just combined. The more you mix this the tougher the topping will be, and you want this really light, so don't overdo it.

Remove the blueberries from the oven, but leave the oven turned on. Divide the dough into 8 equal pieces and place on top of the hot filling, leaving a little space between them. Combine the sugar and cinnamon for the crunch and sprinkle each mound of dough evenly with the cinnamon sugar.

Bake for 15–18 minutes, rotating the pie dish halfway through baking, until the filling is bubbling and the topping is golden brown and cooked through. Transfer the dish to a wire rack and leave to cool for 15 minutes, then serve warm with loads of ice cream.

A number of traditionally British Christmas foods can be traced far back into history. For example, the humble mince pie is rooted in flavours brought back by European Crusaders from the Middle East in the late 11th century. Made with pigeon, hare or mutton, then mixed with fruit, spice and sugar, "Christmas pyes" as they were then called were originally much larger and oblong in shape, thought to represent Jesus's manger. The recipe gradually developed over the years, and by the Victorian era mince pies became smaller, rounder and sweeter. This combination of meat, spices and fruit are tastes that are now inextricably evocative of Christmas time. Love them or loathe them, for me the festive season doesn't officially kick off until I've wolfed down my first mince pie. In fact, my sisters and I hold an annual competition to see who can consume the most mince pies throughout December. I can't lie, the numbers have been pretty impressive in recent years...

The word "Yule" actually derives from a Saxon word meaning midwinter. It was a Nordic tradition to burn a Yule log in the fire over the 12 days of Christmas, and it was considered unlucky to let the log go out during this time. Happily you can avoid this particular stress nowadays, and fulfill Yule log desires by baking my delicious Chocolate & Salted Caramelized Chestnut Yuletide Log – a cracking recipe.

I'm sure most of us hold memories associated with baking as children. My very first memory of cooking is making jam tarts with my mum when I was tiny. There is something magical in how simple, raw ingredients such as flour, eggs and sugar transform unrecognizably after a short time in the oven, more than any other ingredients. All the recipes in this chapter are straightforward and are great for getting the kids involved. My niece is fast becoming a little master baker, and watching her reminds me of when I was first discovering my fascination with cooking.

I think people get put off Christmas baking because of the sense that to do it properly you have to start preparing months in advance, and that kind of insane planning doesn't really fit in with our modern way of living. Christmas baking should be a combination of working with the classics, but also being playful or using modern twists, such as my Dense Chocolate Christmas Cake or my Little Steamed Gilded Ginger Sponge Puddings that can be made in a hour as an alternative to traditional Christmas pudding.

Most of us have a little break from work before Christmas, so I want to encourage you all to take a little time out to try one or two of these recipes and get that Christmas feeling!

Festive
Baking

DENSE CHOCOLATE CHRISTMAS CAKE

The first chocolate fruit cake I ever saw was Nigella Lawson's, about ten years ago and I couldn't quite get my head around it – it was a classic case of "don't judge a book by its cover". It was delicious (a real revelation) – so dense and moist, with stacks of fruit, and the chocolate just added to the body of it. So here is my version, Christmassed-up with more chocolate-friendly dried fruits such as cherries and orange, soaked in chocolate stout and orange liqueur, then wrapped in marzipan and white modelling chocolate (see photograph on page 81). If you're not a classic Christmas cake fan but want to really give it a go, this could be the one to sway you.

For the cake

175g (6oz) unsalted butter, at room temperature, plus extra to butter the tin

350g (12oz) prunes, pitted and roughly chopped

350g (12oz) dried cherries

50g (1¾oz) piece of candied orange peel

80ml (2¾fl oz) maple syrup

150ml (5fl oz) chocolate stout

50ml (2fl oz) Cointreau or Grand Marnier

juice and finely grated zest of 2 oranges

4 tablespoons cocoa powder

3 large free-range eggs, beaten

150g (5½oz) plain flour

175g (6oz) dark brown muscovado sugar

75g (2¾oz) ground almonds

½ teaspoon baking powder

½ teaspoon bicarbonate of soda

4 tablespoons marmalade with no bits, or apricot jam

Butter the sides and base of a loose-bottomed cake tin 20cm (8 inches) in diameter and 9cm (3½ inches) deep, and line with a double layer of baking parchment. Wrap the outside of the tin in baking parchment, this time making it higher than the sides of the cake tin, and tie it in place with kitchen twine. This will insulate the tin, to prevent the sides of the cake from scorching.

Place the butter, fruits, peel, syrup, stout, Cointreau, orange juice and zests and cocoa into a large wide saucepan and bring to a low simmer, stirring until the butter melts. Cook for 10 minutes, then leave to stand for 30 minutes.

Meanwhile, preheat the oven to 170°C/150°C fan (325°F), Gas Mark 3.

Take about one-third of the cake mixture and blend in a food processor until it has turned to a pulp.

Transfer the remaining mixture to a very large mixing bowl. Add the purée, the eggs, flour, sugar, ground almonds, baking powder and bicarbonate of soda, and stir quickly and with confidence until combined.

Pour the fruit cake mixture into the prepared cake tin and bake for 1¾–2 hours. The cake will be slightly sticky and if you insert a skewer into the centre it may still be a little gooey.

Let the cake cool for 15 minutes in the tin, then turn out on to a cooling rack and let it cool completely before wrapping in clingfilm and popping into a cake tin. I think it should be left to mature for a month in a cool place, but it can be eaten straight away.

For the marzipan

500g (1lb 2oz) ground almonds

225g (8oz) caster sugar

225g (8oz) icing sugar

½ teaspoon vanilla extract

1 teaspoon almond extract

4 teaspoons brandy or rum (optional)

juice of 1 lemon

2 free-range eggs, lightly beaten

To decorate

1kg (2lb 4oz) white modelling
   chocolate

decorations of your choice

Decorating is up to you. It can be decorated like a classic fruit cake with a layer of warmed, sieved marmalade or apricot jam, then a layer of marzipan and then a layer of modelling chocolate. I would use the white stuff, as it's Christmas, but brown modelling chocolate is really cool too. And use whatever decorations you fancy – I think the simpler the better for Christmas.

To make the marzipan, mix all the ingredients together and knead until smooth. If the mixture feels too wet, add more ground almonds gradually until it is easier to handle. Roll out between 2 sheets of clingfilm to just over 5mm (¼ inch) thick and about 38cm (15 inches) across. Remove the top sheet of clingfilm, then place your hand under the bottom sheet and quickly upturn the marzipan on to your pre-jammed cake. Smooth and shape the marzipan tightly around the cake, then trim and smooth around the base. Leave the cake under a clean cloth so that the surface of the marzipan can dry a little bit before topping.

To top the cake using white modelling chocolate, put the ready-made paste into the microwave for 10–20 seconds only, or just enough to make it more malleable. Roll out the paste between two sheets of clingfilm as thinly as possible (about 2.5mm/⅛ inch thick) and large enough to completely cover the cake and sides. Remove the top sheet of clingfilm, then place your hand under the bottom sheet and quickly upturn the icing on to your marzipan-covered cake. Smooth it tightly around the cake and either make ruffles around the base or smooth it and trim the excess. Decorate with figurines of your choice, or use the trimmings to make pretty shapes or cut-outs.

GINGERBREAD LATTE CAKE

My mate John Whaite, who won *Great British Bake Off* in 2012, is a fantastic baker and has let me feature his recipe for Gingerbread Latte Cake. This is a really Christmassy cake, but one with quite a modern vibe. My tip would be to NOT EAT all the frosting before frosting the cake. This is easier than it sounds – it has condensed milk in it, for crying out loud!

250g (9oz) unsalted butter, at room temperature, plus extra to butter the tins

225g (8oz) dark muscovado sugar

120g (4¼oz) golden syrup

50g (1¾oz) black treacle

6 large free-range eggs

340g (11¾oz) self-raising flour

1 teaspoon baking powder

1 teaspoon bicarbonate of soda

¼ teaspoon salt

2 teaspoons ground ginger

1 teaspoon ground cinnamon

½ teaspoon freshly ground nutmeg

For the frosting

60g (2¼oz) unsalted butter, at room temperature

200g (7oz) sweetened condensed milk

2 teaspoons instant espresso powder

¼ teaspoon salt

500g (1lb 2oz) mascarpone cream cheese

Preheat the oven to 200°C/180°C fan (400°F), Gas Mark 6. Butter 3 x 20cm (8 inch) sandwich tins, and line the bases with baking parchment.

Beat the butter and muscovado sugar until smooth and fluffy – make sure you beat all the lumps out of the sugar. Beat in the golden syrup, treacle and eggs until reasonably smooth, then sift over the flour, baking powder, bicarbonate of soda, salt and spices, and fold into a smooth batter.

Divide the batter between the 3 cake tins as evenly as possible and bake for 20–25 minutes, or until a skewer inserted into the centre comes out clean. Allow the cakes to cool for 5 minutes in their tins, then invert on to a wire rack to finish cooling.

For the frosting, use an electric hand whisk to beat together the butter and condensed milk until fairly fluffy – about 2 minutes. Add the espresso powder and salt and beat in, then beat in the mascarpone until you have a very smooth, fairly thick frosting.

Once the cakes have cooled, very carefully slice each cake in half horizontally so that you have 6 thin slices of cake. The best way to do this is to place a cake on the worktop, one hand flat on top of it. With a long and sharp serrated knife, score a mark all the way around the edge of the cake as evenly as possible. Use that score mark to guide your knife all the way through the cake, sawing very gently but confidently.

Set a layer of cake aside for the crumb finish. Take the other 5 layers and start to assemble. Place 1 layer on a plate or cake stand, spread it with frosting and repeat until you have 5 slices of cake sandwiched together. Chill for 10 minutes, then spread the remaining frosting around the entire cake as neatly as possible. Make a swirly pattern on the top if you like.

Crumble the reserved layer of cake into small crumbs, then, with a slightly cupped hand, press them around the sides and top edge of the cake. If any frosting peeks through, just cover it with crumbs.

ORANGE EARL GREY MINCE PIES

This pastry will change the way you view mince pies. The Earl Grey infuses into the pastry, giving just a hint of flavour that really brings out the fruit and spices in your mincemeat. If the idea freaks you out, this pastry recipe also works with just the orange zest, and if you like an even simpler pastry you can ditch both the flavourings, but I recommend giving it a go just the once – I'm confident you won't go back. Serve these mince pies with shedloads of cream, brandy cream or brandy butter – or all three. (See photographs on pages 86–7.)

3 tablespoons boiling water

½ teaspoon loose Earl Grey tea

2 tablespoons ice-cold orange juice

2 free-range eggs

225g (8oz) plain flour

a pinch of salt

finely grated zest of 1 orange

125g (4½oz) fridge-cold unsalted butter, cubed

1 x 400g (14oz) jar of mincemeat (or either recipe on page 98 or 99)

30g (1oz) caster sugar, for sprinkling

icing sugar, for dusting

Pour the boiling water over the tea leaves and leave to infuse and cool – keep in the fridge until ready to use.

Beat the orange juice with 1 of the eggs and set aside.

Put the flour into a food processor with the salt and orange zest and whizz for a few seconds. This is a great way of ditching the arduous process of sifting the flour. Add the butter and whizz again for about 20 seconds, or until the mixture resembles breadcrumbs.

Turn out into a fridge-cold mixing bowl (I know this sounds crazy, but it helps prevent the butter melting) and with a cold knife mix in 1 tablespoon of the orange juice and egg mixture, and the cold tea. This will just about bind the mixture together. You may need up to 3 tablespoons of the orange and egg mixture, but the right texture will just form a firm pastry and should feel like it almost needs a little more liquid.

Bind the pastry into a ball. Kneading the pastry at all will make it tough, so really try to handle it as little as possible. Lay the pastry on a baking tray and roll it out to flatten a little. (This makes it easier to roll out completely later on.) Wrap with clingfilm and leave in the fridge to rest for 30 minutes, or until you need it.

Preheat the oven to 220°C/200°C fan (425°F), Gas Mark 7.

Roll out the pastry to 3mm (⅛ inch) thick on a floured work surface. Using a round cutter (about 10cm/4 inches), cut out 16 bases and place them in muffin trays. Put 1½ tablespoons of mincemeat mixture into each. Beat the remaining egg and use it brush the edge of each pie. Re-roll the pastry, and cut out star shapes as lids for the pies. Alternatively you can cut out 7cm (2¾ inch) round lids and press them on top to seal.

Glaze with the rest of the beaten egg and sprinkle with caster sugar. If you've sealed the lids, make a small cut in the top of each pie.

Bake the mince pies for 15–20 minutes, or until golden brown. Leave to cool before releasing them from the muffin trays and dusting with icing sugar.

Charades

Christmas isn't Christmas without a family game of charades. Here are a few festive themes to get you started...

- A Charlie Brown Christmas (TV)
- A Christmas Carol (BOOK)
- All I Want For Christmas Is You (SONG)
- Away in a Manger (SONG)
- Deck the Halls (SONG)
- Ding Dong Merrily On High (SONG)
- Driving Home For Christmas (SONG)
- Elf (FILM)
- Frosty The Snowman (SONG)
- Good King Wenceslas (SONG)
- The Grinch (FILM)
- Hark! The Herald Angels Sing (SONG)
- The Holly And The Ivy (SONG)
- Home Alone (FILM)
- I Saw Mommy Kissing Santa Claus (SONG)
- In The Bleak Midwinter (SONG)
- It's A Wonderful Life (FILM)
- Jingle Bell Rock (SONG)
- Jingle Bells (SONG)
- Last Christmas (SONG)
- Little Donkey (SONG)
- Lonely This Christmas (SONG)
- Miracle On 34th Street (FILM)
- The Muppet Christmas Carol (FILM)
- The Nightmare Before Christmas (FILM)
- O Christmas Tree (SONG)
- O Holy Night (SONG)
- O Little Town Of Bethlehem (SONG)
- Rockin' Around The Christmas Tree (SONG)
- Rudolph the Red-Nosed Reindeer (SONG)
- Silent Night (SONG)
- The Snowman (FILM)
- The Twelve Days Of Christmas (SONG)
- White Christmas (FILM)

What/Who Am I?

This is a simple guessing game where players guess the Christmas character or theme by asking questions with "yes" or "no" answers. All you need are some sticky notes and a pen.

Advent Calendar
Angel Gabriel
Baby Jesus
Bing Crosby
Brussels Sprouts
Carols
Christmas Crackers
Christmas Decorations
Christmas Elves
Father Christmas
Gold, Frankincense and Myrrh
Gingerbread Man
Mince Pies
Mistletoe
Nativity Play
The North Pole
Pantomimes
Presents
Santa's Workshop

Scrooge
Stocking
Stuffing
Toys
Tinsel
Three Wise Men
Turkey
The Virgin Mary

CHOCOLATE & SALTED CARAMELIZED CHESTNUT YULETIDE LOG

Chocolate log is great as it is, but this recipe is extra Christmassy – I've pimped the ordinary chocolate cream filling and swapped it for a velvety chestnut cream with hints of salted caramel, then covered it in broken-up chocolate flakes to make it look even more like a real log. The imperative snow look comes from icing sugar, but I like to modernize it by garnishing it with redcurrants and Christmas decorations. My mum even had the CUTEST woodland animals, but if you can't find any you could always get really crafty and make some out of coloured icing or painted marzipan.

For the cake

unsalted butter, to butter the tin

3 large free-range eggs

75g (2¾oz) caster sugar

50g (1¾oz) plain flour

25g (1oz) cocoa powder

For the filling

100g (3½oz) caster sugar

1 x 200g (7oz) vacuum-pack of ready-cooked, peeled chestnuts

80g (3oz) unsalted butter

150ml (5fl oz) double cream, plus 50ml (2fl oz) for the caramel

1 teaspoon seeded vanilla extract

¾ teaspoon salt

To decorate

150ml (¼ pint) double cream

30g (1oz) unsalted butter

150g (5½oz) dark chocolate

2–3 chocolate flake bars, crumbled

icing sugar, for dusting

a stalk of redcurrants or other Christmas decorations such as holly or figurines

Preheat the oven to 170°C/150°C fan (325°F), Gas Mark 3. Butter a shallow 33 x 23cm (13 x 9 inch) rectangular baking tin and line it with baking parchment.

Put the eggs and sugar into a large mixing bowl (or the bowl of a food processor), then use an electric hand whisk to beat for about 7 minutes, or until the mixture is thick enough to leave a ribbon trail when the whisk is lifted out.

Now sift the flour and cocoa over the egg mixture. I don't normally think you need to sift flour, but in this case, because we're dealing with a delicate mousse, you really must. Gently fold them both in. The mixture will lose volume, but you need to try and get the flour and cocoa incorporated as quickly as possible without knocking out the air. Pour into the prepared tin and bake for 12 minutes, or until the mixture bounces back when lightly touched in the centre. Turn the cake out on to a sheet of baking parchment and leave to cool for 15 minutes.

For the filling, you need to make a dry caramel. This is sometimes considered quite a tricky way to make caramel, but I have fewer mistakes making it this way than any other. The trick is to let the caramel cook very slowly and evenly, and you must never stir the pan until all the sugar has melted. Place the sugar in a frying pan and slowly melt it over a medium heat – this will take about 8 minutes. You can shake the sugar around the pan, but never stir it. By the time the sugar melts it will have started to turn a rich golden colour.

RECIPE CONTINUED OVERLEAF

CHOCOLATE & SALTED CARAMELIZED
CHESTNUT YULETIDE LOG CONT...

When it hits a deep mahogany and has tiny imploding bubbles on the surface, quickly whisk in the butter, the 50ml (2fl oz) of double cream, vanilla extract and salt. Toss the chestnuts though the caramel, then, while they are still hot, blitz in a food processor or blender until smooth. Whip the 150ml (5fl oz) of cream until it forms soft peaks, then fold in the chestnut purée mixture.

To make the icing, place the cream, butter and chocolate in a small pan and heat gently, without boiling, stirring until the chocolate has melted. Remove from the heat and stir until smooth, then leave until cold. Chill for 30 minutes, then beat with a whisk until it thickens up to become a really smooth, glossy paste.

Spread the chestnut cream over the top of the cake. Roll the cake up to form a log shape and place seam side down on a serving plate.

Spread the icing over the top and sides of the cake and smear it into the texture of a log. Scatter the crumbled chocolate flakes over the icing, decorate with a stalk of redcurrants (or whatever you choose) then lightly dust with icing sugar to finish.

JOE'S FIGGY STICKY TOFFEE PUDDING

I met Joe Grey when I was working with the Prince's Trust. He was a bright young whipper-snapper who had worked at the restaurant Fifteen under Jamie Oliver's Food Foundation. Joe won a prize to create a menu for a big restaurant and I was his mentor. Now he is doing fantastic things with a pop-up space and street food ventures. This was the pudding we developed together – a sticky toffee pudding but rammed full of figs, making it more figgy than a figgy pudding. It's a grown-up sticky toffee pudding but still has all the best bits from it, and is a great swap for the anti-Christmas-pudding brigade. It's actually just a great pudding, full stop.

85g (3oz) softened unsalted butter, plus extra for the moulds

150g (5½oz) dates, stoned and chopped

150g (5½oz) dried figs, chopped

250ml (9fl oz) black tea, made with 1 teabag

1 teaspoon bicarbonate of soda

175g (6oz) caster sugar

2 large free-range eggs, beaten

175g (6oz) self-raising flour, sifted

1 teaspoon ground mixed spice

finely grated zest of 1 orange

vanilla ice cream, or clotted cream, to serve

For the sauce:

200g (7oz) light muscovado sugar

200g (7oz) unsalted butter

300ml (10fl oz) double cream

Preheat the oven to 200°C/180°C fan (400°F), Gas Mark 6.

Butter 6 individual dariole pudding moulds or ramekins. Place the dates and figs in a small pan and cover with the hot tea. Bring to the boil and cook for 3–4 minutes, until the dates and figs have softened, then stir in the bicarbonate of soda.

Cream together the butter and sugar, then add the eggs, one at a time. Fold in the flour, mixed spice, orange zest and date and fig mixture and set aside.

To make the sauce, put the muscovado sugar, butter and cream into a pan. Place over a low heat until the sugar has dissolved, then whack the heat up and simmer for 3–4 minutes, or until the sauce is a light toffee colour.

Divide half the sauce between your dariole moulds or ramekins, keeping the other half back to be used as a pouring sauce. Fill to 5mm (¼ inch) from the top with the cake mixture. Cover each mould or ramekin with a square of pleated buttered tin foil (the pleat will help the foil to expand once the pudding starts to rise). Secure with string or an elastic band.

Place the puds in a roasting tray and fill to 1.5cm (⅝ inch) with boiling water. The water creates steam and a mighty lift for the puddings. Bake for 20–25 minutes, until the tops are springy and a skewer comes out clean when inserted.

Serve the puddings by removing the foil, tipping them on to a plate and serving with the rest of the warm sauce and a big scoop of vanilla ice cream or clotted cream.

SERVES 12

PREPARATION TIME: 1 HOUR

COOKING TIME: 1 HOUR

JEWISH FESTIVE CHEESECAKE

Every Christmas without fail we have this cheesecake. My mum was brought up on it, her dad was brought up on it, and I presume it carries on even further back from there. With its hints of lemon and booze-infused sultanas and pastry, it's quite something.

For the pastry

175g (6oz) chilled unsalted butter, cut into small pieces, plus 1 teaspoon for buttering the tin

280g (10oz) plain flour, plus extra for dusting

¼ teaspoon sea salt flakes

4 large free-range egg yolks, beaten

2 tablespoons icing sugar

finely grated zest of 1 lemon

5 tablespoons Marsala

2 free-range egg whites, beaten

For the filling

3 tablespoons sultanas

1 tablespoon chopped candied peel

2 tablespoons Marsala

1kg (2lb 4oz) cream cheese or ricotta

140g (5oz) golden caster sugar

2 tablespoons plain flour

¼ teaspoon sea salt flakes

seeds from 1 vanilla pod, or 1 teaspoon vanilla extract (the seedy stuff is best)

finely grated zest and juice of 1 small orange

finely grated zest and juice of 1 lemon

5 free-range egg yolks

Lightly butter a 20cm (8 inch) springform cake tin. To make the pastry, sift the flour and salt into a large bowl. Make a well in the centre of the flour, add the butter and quickly mix it in with your fingers. Add the whisked egg yolks, icing sugar, lemon zest and Marsala and mix until it forms a smooth ball of dough, but do not over-handle or over-mix the dough. Wrap it in clingfilm and refrigerate for 45 minutes or until it is fairly firm.

While the dough is resting, cover the dried fruits for the filling with the Marsala. You only want to give them a quick soak.

Break off one-third of the dough, dust with flour, and return it to the refrigerator until required. Reshape the rest of the dough (the other two-thirds) into a ball and roll out on a floured work surface into a circle approximately 5cm (2 inches) larger than your cake tin. Carefully roll the circle of dough over the rolling pin and place in the tin. Press carefully round the tin to attach the dough to the sides and cut any excess pastry from the sides of the cake tin with a knife.

Preheat the oven to 200°C/180°C fan (400°F), Gas Mark 6. In a mixing bowl, beat the cream cheese or ricotta with the sugar, flour, salt, vanilla, orange and lemon zest and juice and egg yolks with a wooden spoon until well combined. Stir in the sultanas and candied peel and any remaining Marsala.

Spoon the mixture into the raw pastry case and smooth with a spatula. Remove the reserved pastry dough from the refrigerator and roll into a rectangle, approximately 25cm (10 inches) long. With a knife cut into long strips about 1cm (½ inch) wide. Arrange the strips in a lattice pattern over the top of the cake and brush them with the egg white. Try not to paint the cake between the strips. Bake for 50 minutes to 1 hour, until the filling is only just firm to the touch and the pastry is cooked through and golden (I like it a little undercooked on the inside). Place the tin on a cake rack, very gently undo the springform clip and leave to cool. When cold, slide a knife under the cake and ease it on to a large plate. Serve at room temperature in slices, but store it in the fridge.

LITTLE STEAMED GILDED GINGER SPONGE PUDDINGS
(AN ALTERNATIVE CHRISTMAS PUD)

I published this recipe in my book *Skinny Weeks and Weekend Feasts*, but as ginger is so Christmassy and these are so easy to cook they needed to make a reappearance. I have Christmassed them up by "gilding" them with edible gold glitter, stars, or even edible gold foil to make them really jazzy. If you like a golden syrup-style pud rather than a Christmas pudding, this is the one for you.

150g (5½oz) unsalted butter, at room temperature, plus extra for buttering the moulds

130g (4¾oz) golden caster sugar

3 free-range eggs

150g (5½oz) self-raising flour

a pinch of salt

½ teaspoon baking powder

40g (1½oz) fresh white breadcrumbs

3 tablespoons milk, plus extra if needed

2 tablespoons chopped stem ginger, plus 2 tablespoons of the gingery syrup from the jar

finely grated zest and juice of 1 lemon

edible gold glitter, foil or stars, to decorate

clotted cream, to serve

For the syrup

25ml (1fl oz) ginger liqueur

juice of 1 lemon

4 tablespoons golden syrup

4 tablespoons gingery syrup from the jar of stem ginger (see above)

Preheat the oven to 220°C/200°C fan (425°F), Gas Mark 7. Cream together the butter and sugar using an electric hand mixer and whisk until pale and fluffy. Add the eggs 1 at a time, whisking well after each, then sift over the flour, salt and baking powder and mix to form a batter. Add the breadcrumbs, milk, ginger, syrup, lemon zest and juice and beat together well (the mix should be very creamy – add a little more milk to loosen it if you have to).

Melt together the syrup ingredients in a small pan over a low heat. Butter 8 individual dariole moulds very well and drop 1 tablespoon of the syrup mixture into the base of each. Divide the batter between the moulds. Cover each with a square of pleated buttered foil (the pleat in the middle of the foil will help the foil to expand once the pudding starts to rise) and secure with string.

Place the moulds in a deep roasting tin half filled with hot water. Cook in the oven for 30–35 minutes, until the puddings have puffed up, are firm to the touch and golden on top. Leave to cool slightly, then turn out on to a small plate. Serve sprinkled with gold glitter, foil or stars and a big dollop of clotted cream.

MAKES 1 x 1 LITRE (1¾ PINT) BOTTLE
(ENOUGH FOR 4 BOTTLES OF WINE)
OR 2 X 400ML (14FL OZ) BOTTLES (EACH
ENOUGH FOR 2 BOTTLES OF WINE)

MULLING SYRUP

PREPARATION TIME: 10 MINUTES

COOKING TIME: 5 MINUTES

I bloody love mulled wine. Can't get enough of the stuff – it's not just a sticky hand-warmer to me. Making batches of this syrup will make your life so much easier. And if you package it in cute bottles it makes a terrific gift, to boot. It keeps for 3 months out of the fridge.

400g (14fl oz) caster sugar

400ml (14fl oz) water

2 cinnamon sticks

2 bay leaves

8 black peppercorns

8 cloves

2 star anise

4 allspice berries

pared zest (in strips) and juice of 5 satsumas/mandarins/clementines, or 4 oranges

pared zest (in strips) and juice of 2 lemons

Per bottle of wine

1 bottle of red wine

50ml (2fl oz) brandy

2 clementines (skin on), sliced

2 bay leaves

1 cinnamon stick

Put the sugar, water, cinnamon, bay leaves, peppercorns, cloves, star anise, allspice, zests and juice into a medium saucepan and bring to the boil for 2–3 minutes, then turn the heat off. Strain into a jug, then pour into sterilized glass bottles and put the lids on while still hot, being very careful not to spill any, as boiling sugar is scalding.

Now make the mulled wine (if making as a gift, it's important to write the following instructions on a little tag along with the ingredients, stating how much per bottle of red wine). Mix a quarter of the syrup (for the 1 litre/1¾ pint bottle) or half the syrup (for the 400ml/14fl oz bottles) together with the red wine and brandy in a medium pan. Add the clementines, bay leaves and cinnamon and bring to a simmer. (Make sure you don't bring it to the boil, as the alcohol will disappear.) Leave on a low simmer for a few minutes until the wine has infused all the flavour from the syrup, then strain. Serve immediately.

- MAKES 2KG (4LB 8OZ)
- PREPARATION TIME: 20 MINUTES, PLUS MATURING TIME
- COOKING TIME: NONE

BARNEYS "BLITZ & MIX" MINCEMEAT

My mate Barney Desmazery was my boss when I was at BBC *Good Food*. He's also a terrific cook and a great buddy. His mincemeat technique is the best I've tried. Blitzing half and keeping half chunky makes for a much nicer eat. I've taken his recipe and made it my own with some sour dried pineapple, and it works brilliantly.

50g (1¾oz) blanched almonds

100g (3½oz) chopped candied peel

1 Bramley apple, peeled, cored and chopped into large chunks

50g (1¾oz) stem ginger, plus 2 tablespoons of gingery syrup from the jar

50g (1¾oz) glacé cherries

50g (1¾oz) ready-to-eat dried pineapple

225g (8oz) sultanas

225g (8oz) raisins

225g (8oz) currants

140g (5oz) shredded suet

225g (8oz) light muscovado sugar

¼ teaspoon ground ginger

¼ teaspoon ground mixed spice

¼ teaspoon freshly grated nutmeg

finely grated zest and juice of 1 orange

150ml (5fl oz) Cointreau or brandy

In a food processor, pulse the almonds, candied peel, apple, ginger, cherries and pineapple together until finely chopped (but not mushy), then tip into a large bowl. In batches, pulse the sultanas, raisins and currants until just chopped a little, then add to the bowl.

Sprinkle the suet, sugar and spices over the chopped fruit and mix well, squelching it all through your fingers. Pour over the ginger syrup, orange zest and juice and alcohol, then mix again. Spoon the mixture into sterilized jars and keep until needed. I would give it a good 3 weeks to mature.

MAKES 1.5KG (3LB 5OZ)
OR 5 x 300G (10½OZ) JARS

 PREPARATION TIME: 20 MINUTES,
PLUS MATURING TIME

 COOKING TIME: NONE

SUNNY BLONDE
MINCEMEAT

I just can't compute the amount of people that don't like a minced pie, "Eugh, I don't like raisins..." OK, so fair enough – here I'm offering you an alternative. It's still a mincemeat made of dried fruit. It still works and acts the same inside a buttery pastry crust, but is not too rich or dense. I've taken the pale fruits from the dried fruit counter, tangy and acidic in flavour, and blended them into a mincemeat – they all complement the spices, particularly the mango and pineapple. This recipe needs more liquid than a classic mincemeat because the fruits are a tad drier, but the outcome if used in a mince pie is like the difference between an apricot tart and a dark jam tart (I always thought the sunny orange-coloured ones were the nicest). Really, do give this recipe a go – you mince pie-haters may be convinced that a mince pie is A-OK, and perhaps next year give the real deal another try...?

50g (1¾oz) blanched almonds

100g (3½oz) chopped candied peel

1 Bramley apple, peeled, cored and chopped into large chunks

50g (1¾oz) stem ginger, plus 2 tablespoons of gingery syrup from the jar

150g (5½oz) dried mango

150g (5½oz) dried pineapple

200g (7oz) dried apricots

200g (7oz) dried pear

150g (5½oz) dried apple

200g (7oz) shredded suet

225g (8oz) light muscovado sugar

¼ teaspoon ground ginger

¼ teaspoon freshly grated nutmeg

¼ teaspoon ground cloves

1 rounded teaspoon ground cinnamon

finely grated zest and juice of 2 oranges

finely grated zest and juice of 1 lemon

400ml (14fl oz) Cointreau or brandy

In a food processor, pulse the almonds, candied peel, apple, ginger, mango, pineapple, apricots, pear and dried apple together in batches until finely chopped (but not mushy), then tip into a large bowl.

Sprinkle the suet, sugar and spices over all the chopped fruit and mix well, squelching it through your fingers. Pour over the ginger syrup, orange and lemon juice, zest and alcohol, then mix again. Spoon the mixture into sterilized jars and keep until needed. I would give it a good 3 weeks to mature.

Where's the buffet gone? It agitates me that we only really have them during the winter festive period. How did we get here? I guess we went through a stage of embracing formal dining. With the popularity of celebrity chefs and cooking shows on TV, people are bringing the things even I find ludicrous in restaurants into the home. Going to someone's home and having canapés, then an amuse-bouche, then starters, a main course, dessert and petits fours is my idea of hell. Trust me when I tell you that a Michelin-starred chef does not cook like this at home. This is just showing off. Your guests don't want it. They want to feel comfortable and have your focus. And don't get me started on canapé parties, the ultimate way of "keeping up with the Joneses". As a trainee chef I catered for so many events like this. The same vibe at each... starving people hovering close to the kitchen, never quite getting their fill, and a room filled with people who've drunk too much and not eaten enough. A frantic host (or head chef in my case) never quite being on top of anything... and food that's not as good as proper cooking!

When in my home, I want to eat family-style. Big platters filled with food that you have to help your neighbours to. A vat of something delicious placed on the table for people to fill up on, with a few complementary sides. This is how I prefer to dine... but at Christmas, when I'm entertaining more than 10 people I want a buffet!

A buffet doesn't have to be of the retro kind, with cheese-and-pineapple hedgehogs and depressing soggy sandwiches. I truly believe that laying on a fantastic spread means you can go to town with an opulent and varied array of food. This is a much more practical way to feed larger groups. One of the best weddings I ever went to offered guests a buffet instead of a formal meal. It was beautiful, with a suckling pig, a huge platter of seafood,

amazing salads... There is something so celebratory about seeing a copious display of food in front of you, which you just don't get with formal dining. Indeed, I believe that the secret to a buffet's success lies in this very informality. People can take what they want, and there is something so convivial about helping to serve each other. In this way I really feel it can help create a festive atmosphere.

Also, there are loads of pragmatic advantages to serving a buffet. You will undoubtedly find it cheaper to prepare than a formal meal, as you will be able to feed more people with less food, (while giving you the opportunity to use up leftovers you might have). What's more, much of the work can be done in advance – instead of being stuck in the kitchen between courses, once the buffet's laid out you can be part of the party and relax and enjoy the food with everyone else.

This is not to say you shouldn't try and WOW when doing a buffet by providing a wider variety of tastes while still showcasing great cooking. The key is to have one main focus. As it's Christmas, I'm going to use the Spiced Pineapple Christmas Ham as the main attraction. It then needs a decent terrine – I give you The Creamiest & Lightest Chicken Liver Parfait. Some Quickest Pickled Pineapple to go with each, and a Seafood Platter with the Best Marie Rose Sauce You'll Ever Eat over ice. I take on some buffet classics such as Curried Eggs, a few salads and some carbs in the form of potatoes or simply, good bread. A cheese plate, or charcuterie for the lazy? This is still glam eating, but it's homely and most of all it's FUN! What's not to like? I hereby rest my case for the resurrection of the buffet: bring it out from the Dark Ages and into the modern-day party!

Bring back
the buffet

SERVES 14 AS PART OF A BUFFET, WITH LEFTOVERS

 PREPARATION TIME: 30 MINUTES, PLUS SOAKING OVERNIGHT

 COOKING TIME: 3 HOURS

SPICED PINEAPPLE CHRISTMAS HAM

The Christmas ham. I love it so much. I've written numerous ham recipes in my time – mango-glazed, pomegranate-glazed – if it's got the combo of sweetness, tartness and spice it's going to be a winner. This recipe uses pineapple, and the tartness outweighs its sweetness. I think it cuts through the ham in the most brilliant way.

For the ham

1 x 4kg (9lb) boned and rolled smoked gammon ham (about half a ham), soaked overnight in loads of cold water

3 litres (5¼ pints) pineapple juice (the best-quality pure carton stuff – it's not worth juicing fresh pineapple for this recipe)

2 onions, peeled and quartered

3 carrots, peeled and halved

3 sticks of celery, halved lengthways and widthways

1 Scotch bonnet chilli

1 cinnamon stick

2 star anise

10 allspice berries

10 black peppercorns

a good few thyme sprigs

2 bay leaves

For the glaze

100ml (3½fl oz) pineapple juice

2 tablespoons redcurrant jelly

2 tablespoons unsalted butter

½ teaspoon mixed spice

½ teaspoon smoked paprika

½ teaspoon ground cloves

Find the biggest pot you can in which the ham will fit. Put the ham in the pot, pour in the pineapple juice and top up with water so that the ham is covered. Add the onions, carrots, celery, the chilli, spices and herbs to the pan. Slowly bring the liquid to the boil, removing any scum as it appears until the surface appears clear.

Once the liquid is boiling, reduce the heat to a fast simmer and allow it to bubble away for 1¼ hours, topping up the water level regularly to ensure the ham is fully covered at all times, and removing scum from the surface every time you do so. Once the ham is cooked, remove it from the pan very carefully so as not to tear any of the meat. You may find this easier if you let the ham cool a little in the cooking liquor, then allow it to drain and cool in a colander for 10 minutes. Place the ham in a large roasting tin. Very carefully, carve the skin away to reveal the thick layer of white fat – if you're lucky it will peel away easily – then score the fat so you make loads of slashes all over it, or crossways in both directions to make little diamond shapes if you prefer.

Heat the oven to 240°C/220°C fan (475°F), Gas Mark 9. Put all the glaze ingredients in a pan and simmer until reduced to a syrupy glaze that will stick to the ham. Rub the glaze all over the ham and into the corner of each diamond. Roast for 20–25 minutes, until sticky and caramelized. Leave the ham to rest for 15 minutes if you want to eat it warm, or let it cool completely.

 # Charcuterie board

Charcuterie boards are meant to be simple, as there is no cooking involved, but it's worth paying attention to the details such as presentation and your choices of meat to achieve a delicious, interesting and well-balanced selection that everyone will love. Like a cheese board, you want to have a nice variety – I like to offer both cured and cooked meats. Paté can also be a nice addition. It's worth getting friendly with your local deli who will be able to recommend what's good. And bear in mind that the aim of a charcuterie board is to enjoy a range of different flavours and textures, so be careful not to over-buy – around 60–90g of meat per person should be about right for a starter, and in my bid to bring back the buffet this is a great option. When presenting your board, layer in slices, or shape the finer sliced hams into waves or curls.

CURED (CRUDO)

These are raw meats that have been cured with salt.

Prosciutto A very popular part of any charcuterie board. Parma ham is generally considered the best. You want this sliced as thinly as possible. Otherwise you could go down the Spanish root with some sweet Serrano or Jamón Ibérico.

Bresoala Beef tenderloin that's been air-dried and salted.

Capicola Dry-cured pork shoulder.

Salami or saucisson There is a huge variety here, but essentially we are talking about a peppered or spiced cured and dried sausage. There are a variety of salamis and saucissons from all over Europe, including my beloved sweet, hot chorizo. Alternatively you might want to experiment with a fragrant fennel based *finocchiona*, but for a cool-looking board mix up some of the whole finer sausages with some freshly cut slices of the fatter variety.

'Nduja The super-cool new kid on the block and the spiciest to boot. This is a cured HEAVILY spiced pork paste, and on a charcuterie platter I would spread it simply on grilled hot sourdough and let the fat sink deep into the bread. Its Spanish "cousin" is a little coarser, called *sobrassada*.

Lardo This is a bit naughty but utterly delicious on top of toast with a little sprinkling of sea salt flakes. The best ones are heavy with herbs.

COTTO (COOKED)

These are cooked meats. They are a little less salty than the cured ones so it's nice to have a couple of options here to balance your board.

Cooked ham This might be a good time to use up any baked ham you have left over from Christmas.

Mortadella Large Italian sausage made with finely ground pork, garlic and spices from Bologna.

PATÉ/TERRINE/RILLETTES

These mixes of cooked ground meats in spreadable form are my favourite of the lot. I am happiest sitting at a window writing with some pork rillettes, great sourdough and cornichons, and I've done some of my best work if I have a carafe of really good red wine in tow, too...

Paté Another great textural dimension to add to your charcuterie board. Chicken liver paté is a classic, but try experimenting with other types too, from coarse game-based paté's, duck liver paté, or a really smooth parfait, which I prefer (see page 108).

Terrine This is a coarse layered paté and meat hybrid named after the type of mould or dish in which it's cooked. The real deal is pretty complex and technical to make, but you can make anything in a terrine mould and refer to it as one these days.

Rillettes Duck, goose or pork meat cooked very, very slowly in its own fat until it starts to fall apart and go all shreddy. It's then blitzed until its really shredded, packed into a terrine mould or individual jars and covered in any excess fat in order to preserve it. A scoop of rillettes on a charcuterie board is the first thing I make a beeline for.

Pork pie A traditional British cold meat pie with a coarse pork and pork jelly filling sealed in a hot water crust pastry. This is not technically charcuterie, but I buy a Mrs King's pork pie every year for my charcuterie board. I have made them in the past, but why bother if you can buy a good-quality pork pie?

ACCOMPANIMENTS

You will want some kind of bread (always sourdough for me) to serve with your charcuterie board, whether this is a loaf, little toasts, crackers or bread sticks.

To cut through all the salt, no charcuterie board is complete without something sweet and acidic.

Cornichons and tiny silverskin onions – Cornichons are mini gherkins and THE MOST essential sidekick to your board, and if they come in jars with tiny silverskin onions, then all the better.

Piccalilli I love this British relish of chopped pickled vegetables and spices in all guises. In my book *Gizzi's Healthy Appetite* I featured a recipe for Sophia's Pinkalilli and it's brilliant with charcuterie.

Chutney Go for Christmassy flavoured chutneys such as quince, apple, pear or dried fruits.

PREPARATION TIME: 10 MINUTES, PLUS 1 WEEK PICKLING

COOKING TIME: 5 MINUTES

THE QUICKEST PICKLED PINEAPPLE

This is so simple, and something a bit different. You will end up with a deliciously zingy, spicy accompaniment for your charcuterie board or Christmas ham, or you can get on a '70s trip and eat it cut into chunks with a slightly swankier Montgomery Cheddar cheese, in true pineapple hedgehog style! It also looks lovely on your shelf and makes a great present.

300ml (10fl oz) cider vinegar

200g (7oz) brown sugar

50g (1¾oz) salt

2 bay leaves

1 cinnamon stick

8 whole cloves

2 whole star anise

1 tablespoon pink peppercorns

2 dried whole chillies

5 allspice berries

1 ripe pineapple

Place everything bar the pineapple in a pan and bring to the boil. While the liquor is heating up, prepare your pineapple. Cut off the top and bottom and slice off the skin, then cut into quarters. Cut out the core of each quarter, then slice into further strips. Put the pineapple into a sterilized 1½–2 litre (2¾–3½ pint) kilner jar.

Once the liquor is boiling and the sugar and salt have dissolved, turn off the heat and pour over the pineapple. Make sure the jar is properly sealed, and leave to mature in a cool, dry place for about a week before eating (it's even better after about a month). It'll keep for about 6 months, but I'd be surprised if you don't get through it all over Christmas.

THE CREAMIEST & LIGHTEST CHICKEN LIVER PARFAIT

The difference between a paté and a parfait is in how it's cooked and the inclusion of eggs. A paté is probably easier to make, but it's also easier to get wrong. Even I find it hard to get a smooth bright pink paté, and that's the real aim. With a parfait, you make a shallot reduction, blend it with livers, butter and eggs, then place it in a terrine and cook it very slowly until it's just set. The result is a delightfully light, brilliant pink and super-tasty parfait. There is one step we must talk about. It's the sieving step. I won't beat about the bush: it's grim sieving processed livers, but this step is so crucial to its finish that you just have to bite the bullet, get your mind elsewhere and hope it goes quickly. I do promise, though, that once you've made this, your paté-making will be a thing of the past. A little note: The Quickest Pickled Pineapple (see page 107) and some Crispy Chicken Skin (see page 119) go brilliantly with this recipe.

1kg (2lb 4oz) chicken livers, at room temperature

400g (14fl oz) butter, at room temperature

5 eggs, at room temperature

2 teaspoons sea salt flakes

a massive grinding of black pepper

For the reduction

150ml (5fl oz) brandy

150ml (5fl oz) port

150ml (5fl oz) Madeira

8 small shallots, finely chopped

1 garlic clove

a few thyme sprigs

To serve

toasted sourdough bread

pickle or chutney

Preheat the oven to 140°C/120°C fan (275°F), Gas Mark 1.

First you need to make your shallot reduction. Place all the reduction ingredients in a small pan and bring to the boil. Reduce the liquid until there is almost none left and the shallots are soft. Remove the thyme sprigs, then place the shallot reduction with all the remaining ingredients in a blender or food processor and blend until smooth.

Pass the mixture through a fine sieve and transfer to a 2-litre (3½ pint) ovenproof terrine mould. Fill it no higher than 5mm (¼ inch) from the top. Tap the full mould on your worktop to knock out any air bubbles. Place a sheet of baking parchment over the top of the mixture and wrap in foil. Place the mould in a deep roasting dish and pour water into the dish to come halfway up the sides of the mould, to create a bain marie in which to gently cook the parfait. Bake for 25 minutes, then turn the mould around and bake for a further 25 minutes. Remove the foil and baking parchment. The parfait should be just set and should only move a little when touched, like jelly (if not set, cook for a further 5 minutes). Leave to cool, then place the parfait in the fridge for 12 hours to set.

To serve, you need 2 spoons the same size. The top will have oxidized and you can scrape this off, but I don't bother. Plunge the spoons into boiling water and scrape against the surface of the parfait. You want to create a perfect egg shape. If you find it hard with just one spoon, use the second spoon to scrape against the first in order to make an egg(ish) shape. Serve with toasted sourdough, some kind of sweet pickle or chutney and extra salt and pepper to taste.

SERVES 8 AS A STARTER OR
AS PART OF A BUFFET

PREPARATION TIME: 25 MINUTES,
PLUS COOLING

COOKING TIME: 30 MINUTES

SEAFOOD PLATTER
WITH THE BEST MARIE ROSE SAUCE YOU'LL EVER EAT

I'm going out on a limb here by saying that most people in the country will be starting their Christmas lunch with either prawn cocktail or smoked salmon. It's a sweeping statement, I know, but even if you don't have it on the big day, chances are you will at some point over the festive period. I featured my ultimate avocado prawns recipe in *Gizzi's Healthy Appetite* and what made the sauce so great was that I used a roasted prawn oil and ditched cayenne and Tabasco for sriracha and Korean chilli powder. I'm featuring it here again because it can't be beaten, but this time with a different serving suggestion – having it as a dip with whole prawns, as a platter for a starter or as part of a canapé party or, even better, a buffet (I'm still on a massive campaign to bring back the buffet!). I've suggested a mixture of seafood such as large shell-on prawns, crab claws and some of those small sweet Atlantic prawns, but you can just serve large prawns. (See photograph on page 111.)

a mixture of different shellfish including large raw shell-on prawns, the right size for plunging, plus crab claws and small Atlantic prawns (alternatively, use approximately 30 large raw shell-on prawns)

ice cubes, to serve

lemon wedges, to serve

For the Marie Rose sauce

200ml (7fl oz) vegetable oil

2 super-fresh free-range egg yolks

1 teaspoon Dijon mustard

1 tablespoon sherry vinegar

150ml (5fl oz) extra virgin olive oil

2 tablespoons lemon juice

2 tablespoons tomato ketchup

1 tablespoon tomato purée

1 teaspoon brandy

2 teaspoons sriracha chilli sauce

1 teaspoon Korean chilli powder, to garnish

sea salt flakes and freshly ground black pepper

First, make your roasted prawn oil. Peel the prawns and put the shells and heads to one side and the prawns tails to the other. Heat the vegetable oil in a saucepan. Add the prawn shells and heads and start to fry them. To begin with loads of liquid will come out of the shells, but then it will begin to evaporate and the prawn shells will start to fry. Keep bashing the heads to get all the juice out of them and fry for about 3–4 minutes, or until the shells go lightly golden. Leave to cool for 20 minutes to infuse the oil, then strain through a fine sieve. Throw out the shells and leave the oil to cool to room temperature.

Making a court-bouillon to cook your prawns (and crab claws if using) will bring out their sweetness. In a ginormous stockpot over a medium-high heat, add all the court-bouillon ingredients and bring to the boil. Reduce the heat and simmer for 20 minutes. The aromatics will infuse the wine and water and make a really delicious stock. Drop your prawns and crab claws into the boiling stock and poach for 1½ minutes, or until just cooked through but still opaque in the middle. Drain, then plunge them into iced water to cool them down quickly. Remove the stock vegetables and place the prawns and crab on a tray lined with kitchen paper. Leave to cool to room temperature, then wrap them in clingfilm and leave in the fridge until ready to use.

For the court-bouillon (optional, alternatively just use 3 tablespoons of salted water)

2 litres (3½ pints) cold water

400ml (14fl oz) dry white wine

1 garlic bulb

1 onion, sliced

2 sticks of celery with leaves, sliced

2 carrot, roughly chopped

1 lemon, sliced

2 bay leaves

a good few thyme sprigs

a good few parsley sprigs

2½ tablespoons Old Bay seasoning

3 tablespoons sea salt flakes

To make the Marie Rose sauce, place the yolks, Dijon mustard, vinegar and some seasoning in a mixing bowl, then combine the the olive oil and the prawn oil in a jug. With an electric whisk, beat the egg mixture and very slowly trickle the oils in. It will take a few seconds before the mayonnaise starts to emulsify. Keep trickling the oil in until half of it has been used up, by which stage the mayo should be stable and you can speed up the pouring until combined. You want a thick wobbly mayonnaise. Season with the lemon juice, salt and pepper. Mix the ketchup, tomato purée, brandy and sriracha with the mayonnaise to make the sauce. It will now have a thick, but coatable consistency. Pop it into a bowl and sprinkle over the Korean chilli powder. Lay the ice cubes on a large serving platter and place the Marie Rose sauce in the centre. Scatter the prawns or seafood around, plonk on some lemon wedges and you are ready to serve.

ROASTED PORCINI
WITH BURRATA
& PICKLED WALNUTS

When we consider indulgent food we tend to imagine meat or seafood, but some of the most decadent of all grow right out of the ground. Porcini mushrooms or ceps (whichever you want to call them) are the King of mushrooms. They have a short season and are few and far between, so can be quite pricey, but for their meaty, dirty, fragrant flavour it's worth it. Pan-roasting a few of these in garlic and parsley to just serve simply on a plate is a joy; to make them a bit more "fancy", serve your porcini at room temperature, adding some pickled walnuts and a heaving ball of oozing burrata cheese to scoop on to garlic butter croutes as a starter, canapé or part of a buffet. Alternatively you can serve the porcini with really cheesy wet polenta as a fantastic vegetarian main course.

3 tablespoons unsalted butter

3 tablespoons good olive oil

700g (1lb 9oz) nice big fresh porcini mushrooms, cleaned and trimmed, each sliced into 4 along the stalk

2–3 garlic cloves, very finely chopped

2 tablespoons finely chopped flat-leaf parsley leaves

3–4 pickled walnuts, roughly chopped

3 small balls of burrata, left to get to room temperature, drained and dried with kitchen paper

really good extra virgin olive oil, for finishing

micro parsley or flat leaf parsley, to garnish

sea salt flakes and freshly ground black pepper

Heat the butter and oil in a very large frying pan. When the pan is roasting hot and the butter is foaming, add the mushrooms in batches and fry until heavily bronzed. When they're all done, put them back into the pan along with any juices (they should all fit now they've been cooked and lost their water content), add the garlic, stir in the parsley and season heavily with salt and pepper. Lay on a serving platter and leave to get to room temperature, which doesn't actually take that long.

Sprinkle over the chopped walnuts and, if you like a little more zing, 1 tablespoon of the vinegar they've been pickled in. Add the balls of burrata to the platter – you can keep them whole or tear into them a bit. Season with more salt and pepper, garnish with parsley and drizzle with good olive oil to serve.

SALT POTATOES
WITH FOUR DIPS

My mate Rose introduced these to me and they are THE easiest and most perfect party food of all time. This way of cooking potatoes is traditionally from Columbia, South Carolina, where a variety of different types of potatoes are readily available. Needless to say you could do this with just one type, but choosing a variety looks so festive and who doesn't love a purple potato? The trick is to make sure that they are all similar in size. Great as part of a buffet or canapé feast. I've given you four dips that I think work wonders, but you can play around with whatever you fancy.

3kg (6lb 8oz) mixed (white-skinned, red-skinned and purple-skinned) small potatoes, left whole

3.5 litres (5¾ pints) water

150g (5½oz) fine sea salt

Place the potatoes in a large pan and pour over the water. Add the salt and stir, then bring to the boil with a lid on. Once boiling, remove the lid and boil for 45 minutes, or until the water has evaporated and the potatoes are crystallized with salt. Tip them out into a colander and allow to steam for 10 minutes before serving on a platter with dips.

SOURED CREAM, EGG, CHIVES & CAVIAR

Empty a 300g (10½oz) tub of soured cream into a bowl and top with 1 grated hard-boiled egg, ½ a small packet (about 15g/½oz) of fresh chives, finely chopped, and whatever caviar you can afford – I would go for 100g (3½oz). Lumpfish roe is totally great with this, too. When I make this for an event I crumble over some finely chopped Crispy Chicken Skin (see page 119) as well.

SALSA VERDE

In a food processor blitz 1–2 garlic cloves, a small handful of drained pickled capers, a small handful of drained cornichons, 6 anchovy fillets, 2 handfuls of flat-leaf parsley, a handful of basil leaves, a handful of mint leaves, 1 teaspoon of Dijon mustard, 3 tablespoons of sherry vinegar, the juice of ½ lemon, 150ml (5fl oz) of extra virgin olive oil and some salt and pepper.

SOURED CREAM, CHIVES & CRISPY BACON

Empty a 300g (10½oz) tub of soured cream into a bowl and top with ½ a small packet (about 15g/½oz) of fresh chives, finely chopped, and 100g (3½oz) of very thinly sliced smoked streaky bacon that's been fried to a crisp.

CRÈME FRAÎCHE, HARISSA & CHOPPED PRESERVED LEMONS

Empty a 300g (10½oz) tub of crème fraîche into a serving bowl. Top with 1 tablespoon of harissa, 1 preserved lemon, very thinly sliced, then finely chopped, and 1 tablespoon of dill.

* SERVES 12 AS PART OF A BUFFET
  OR 6 AS A STARTER
* PREPARATION TIME: 50 MINUTES
  IF MAKING CRISPY CHICKEN SKIN,
  10 MINUTES, PLUS COOLING IF NOT
* COOKING TIME: 40 MINUTES IF MAKING
  CRISPY CHICKEN SKIN, 10 MINUTES IF NOT

CURRIED EGGS

The easiest but most delicious of all party foods. Some traditional recipes you don't want to mess with, and this is one of them – all I've done differently is top them with herbs, some of which might not be the usual contenders for curry, but still work remarkably well with these eggs. The best tip I would give is to make some Crispy Chicken Skin, roughly chop it and use as a topping, too.

12 free-range eggs (I use Cotswold Legbars or Burford Browns for their orange yolks)

6 tablespoons mayonnaise

1 tablespoon crème fraîche

1 tablespoon English mustard, plus extra to garnish

1 tablespoon curry powder

sea salt flakes and freshly ground black pepper

For the crispy chicken skin

325g (11½oz) chicken skin (you can get this from a butcher, or save it when cooking chicken and freeze it over time)

a decent sprinkling of sea salt flakes

To garnish

a few mint leaves

a few dill or fennel fronds, torn

1 tablespoon very finely chopped chives (optional)

To make the Crispy Chicken Skin (if using), heat the oven to 200°C/180°C fan (400°F), Gas Mark 6 and line 2 baking sheets with baking parchment.

Spread out the chicken skin in a flat single layer on the baking sheets and season lightly with salt. Top the chicken skin with another sheet of baking parchment and place another baking sheet or tray on top to weight it down. Bake for 20–30 minutes, until the skins are golden and crisp, rotating the baking sheets from front to back and top to bottom halfway through baking. Remove and dry on kitchen paper. Store in an airtight container on more baking parchment until ready to use.

To make the eggs, lower the eggs gently into a pan of boiling water and boil for 8–9 minutes. Remove, run under a cold tap and peel. The sooner you peel them, the easier they are to do.

Dry the eggs with kitchen paper and carefully cut them in half. Scoop out the yolks (try to avoid splitting the whites) and pop them into a mixing bowl. Lay the whites on a serving platter ready to be filled again with the curry mayonnaise you're about to make. Mash the yolks until they become the texture of fine crumbs. Mix in the mayonnaise, crème fraîche, mustard and curry powder and whisk until it's all combined – it will be bright yellow. You can give it a quick whizz in a small blender if you want it really smooth.

Now it's time to fill the whites. You can do this in two ways: with 2 teaspoons, or by doing it the old-school way with a piping bag. I pipe! It just looks cooler and more retro and you have more control. Fill each of the egg white halves evenly until all the filling is used up. You can be surprisingly generous with the filling. Finally, sprinkle over the herbs and, if you're using it, some finely chopped Crispy Chicken Skin, scatter with seasoning and serve.

PARMESAN SNOWFLAKES
WITH GOATS' CHEESE MOUSSE
& PICKLED BEETROOT

I have a huge disdain for canapés, so the introduction of these, which are undoubtedly finger food, may seem a bit of a contradiction, BUT I had to include them. Cooking Parmesan in rounds in the oven makes the most beautiful lacy snowflake-like bases that are brilliant for garnishing food but also scream out to be topped. A really light goats' cheese mousse and some home-pickled beetroot sit on top in a delicious mish-mash of flavours, colours and textures, and… well… they do look like snowflakes and that's just TOO CHRISTMASSY to ignore.

For the pickled beetroot

250ml (9fl oz) white wine
  or cider vinegar

100g (3½oz) golden caster sugar

30g (1oz) sea salt flakes

1 thyme sprig

a pinch of chilli flakes

3 purple beetroots (or 1 purple,
  1 golden and 1 candy), peeled
  and cut into small (about 8mm/
  ⅜ inch), dice

For the goats' cheese mousse

220g (8oz) chèvre (firm goats'
  cheese)

100ml (3½fl oz) double cream

1 teaspoon truffle oil (optional but
  TOTALLY recommended)

½ teaspoon really finely ground
  black pepper

For the Parmesan crisps

a few thyme sprigs, leaves picked and
  chopped

120g (4¼oz) Parmesan cheese,
  freshly grated

To garnish

chopped chervil and/or dill

First make the pickled beetroot. Heat the vinegar, sugar, salt, thyme and chilli in a saucepan until the sugar has melted. Add the beetroot and simmer for 10 minutes, then leave aside to cool to room temperature.

To make the mousse, blend the goats' cheese, cream, truffle oil (if using), salt and plenty of freshly ground black pepper in a food processor until smooth and light. Transfer to a piping bag.

For the Parmesan crisps, preheat the oven to 190°C/170°C fan (375°F), Gas Mark 5. Line a baking tray with baking parchment. Mix together the thyme and Parmesan, then sprinkle on to the baking parchment in rounds, about 3cm (1¼ inch) in diameter and a couple of millimetres (¹⁄₁₆ inch) thick. Bake in the oven for 10 minutes, then remove and allow to cool on the tray. You'll need to do this in batches to get the full 24 – you'll probably get 9–12 on each baking tray.

Just before you want to serve them, construct the canapés: lay the Parmesan discs on a large but low-rimmed serving platter. Pipe a little of the goat's cheese mousse on to each disc, and top with a small amount, maybe ½–¾ teaspoon, of the pickled beetroot. Sprinkle a little chervil or dill over the top and try not to eat them all before your guests have a chance.

OMBRASSICA SALAD
WITH CHILLI & ANCHOVY DRESSING

Roasting brassicas gets the best out of them. It concentrates their flavour, brings out their sweetness, and stops them from becoming "soggy" or "cabbagey". This is an all-round win, which is probably why the world is going berserk for brassicas. So, in a classic ombré white-to-dark-green colour palette, I've taken my favourite brassicas and roasted them for a seasonal salad. Any leftovers are brilliant heated up and topped with a couple of fried eggs.

For the salad

1 head of broccoli, cut into florets

1 cauliflower, cut into florets

1 Romanesco cauliflower, cut into florets

350g (12oz) Brussels sprouts, cut in half

1 bunch of purple-sprouting broccoli, woody stalk ends removed

3 tablespoons rapeseed or olive oil

sea salt flakes and freshly ground black pepper

For the dressing

6 tablespoons golden rapeseed or extra virgin olive oil

2 garlic cloves, finely chopped

2 red chillies, finely chopped

12 anchovy fillets (leave them out if you're not a fan, but trust in their saltiness, not fishiness)

2–3 tablespoons freshly squeezed lemon juice

½ small bunch (about 15g/½oz) fresh parsley, leaves picked

Preheat the oven to 220°C/200°C fan (425°F), Gas Mark 7. Arrange the brassicas in colour order from light to dark on a roasting tray (or 2 trays if they don't all fit in a single layer). Coat with the oil and a little salt. Roast in the oven for 15–20 minutes, depending on how al dente you like them, giving them a little shake and toss halfway through the cooking.

To make the dressing, heat the oil, garlic, chillies and anchovy fillets in a pan and allow everything to cook slowly over a low heat until it's all fizzing away and the garlic is cooked but not golden or bitter. Add the lemon juice and parsley and take off the heat. Whisk with a sauce whisk until emulsified, then season with loads of black pepper and a spot of salt.

Lay the roasted brassicas on a platter in light to dark ombré order. Pour over the dressing and leave to get to room temperature before serving.

A GREAT SALAD FOR ANY TIME OVER THE HOLIDAYS

Does what it says on the tin. Brilliant with so many things.

1 teaspoon Dijon mustard

1 teaspoon honey

1 tablespoon sherry vinegar

a squeeze of lemon juice

6 tablespoons really good extra virgin olive oil, or a blend of extra virgin olive oil and golden rapeseed oil

2 Little Gem lettuces

1 red endive

1 white endives

1 bunch of watercress

12 radishes, thinly sliced

3 spring onions, cut into matchsticks and left in iced water for 5 minutes

a small handful of fresh mint leaves, thinly sliced (optional)

sea salt flakes and freshly ground black pepper

Whisk together the mustard, honey, vinegar, lemon juice and seasoning, then very slowly whisk in the oil until combined. It will be a glittering gold colour.

Separate the salad leaves, wash them in ice-cold water and dry them in a salad whizzer or on kitchen paper. Pop them on to a platter or a salad bowl and drizzle over the dressing. Finally mix in the radishes, spring onions and mint and serve straight away.

In this chapter I've taken inspiration from European Christmas Eve traditions. In countries such as Italy, Poland and Spain, celebrations on December 24th take precedence over any other in the Christmas calendar. Midnight Mass, a communion service held at midnight to mark the birth of Jesus, usually follows a feast of some description. Christmas Eve is traditionally a day reserved for fasting and abstinence, which is rewarded with an extravagant, but commonly meatless, meal at the end of the day. Across many different cultures, this meal only begins once the first star can be seen in the Noel night sky. In Poland, the Christmas Eve meal is called the *Wigilia*, derived from the Latin phrase, "to watch", and the table will often be laid with a crisp white tablecloth to represent Christ's purity and his swaddling clothes. There is a long held Southern Italian Christmas Eve tradition of the "Feast of Seven Fishes", which I have made reference to in my recipes for Smoke-roasted Treacle-cured Salmon, Salmon en Croute and Buttery Whole Baked Haddock. If nothing else I think it's a lovely idea to eat fish before the meat mania that ensues over the following days.

One tradition we Erksines have developed is eating a really authentic Italian Veal Milanese on the night before Christmas. I don't really know where this came from, but it's a really simple and satisfying supper that takes a break from all the heavy spicing of classic Christmas food. In the UK, the Christmas Day lunch is the main event, but I think you still want something special the night before, just with maybe a little less washing-up and fuss. This way you can afford yourself some time to go about any other preparations for the days ahead in a relaxed manner, (or not if there is last-minute present buying to deal with!).

It's also a time to prepare for the days ahead. We always put our Christmas ham in to soak on Christmas Eve ready for Boxing Day, and there's lots of little things that can be done to make the day itself go without a hitch.

Once I tweeted to ask what people ate on Christmas Eve. I was shocked to discover that lots of people were eating soup. When I asked why, many responded by saying it was how they prepared themselves for the amount of eating anticipated the following day. Others were eating buffet-style and preparing a large ham for Christmas Eve. We used to do the same when my mum had an annual Erskine Christmas Eve party which always involved a whole baked smoked gammon with a whole baked fish, new potatoes and salad.

To me, Christmas is all about making your own personal family traditions, and I hope this chapter will give you some fresh ideas that you'll want to return to year after year.

The night
before
Christmas

CHICKEN & GIROLLE PITHIVIER

A pithivier sounds posh, but it's really a flat pie to you and me. Chicken pie is my little sister Cora's favourite food, so it's one I've absolutely mastered. This season you don't really get better than girolle mushrooms, but you could swap them for simple chestnut mushrooms if you prefer. And the truffle… well, that's optional, but it is Christmas Eve, after all…

1 small whole chicken

1 onion

2 carrots

2 sticks of celery

10 peppercorns

1 bay leaf

a few thyme sprigs

a few rosemary sprigs

30g (1oz) unsalted butter

30g (1oz) plain flour, plus extra for dusting

150ml (5fl oz) good-quality cider

250ml (9fl oz) chicken stock

50ml (2fl oz) double cream

50g (1¾oz) Parmesan cheese, freshly grated

1 tablespoon olive oil

150g (5½oz) girolle mushrooms

2 garlic cloves, finely chopped

2 x 320g (11½ oz) packets of ready-rolled all-butter puff pastry

1 free-range egg, beaten

sea salt flakes and freshly ground black pepper

Place the whole chicken in a big stockpot and cover with water. Add the onion, carrots, celery, peppercorns and herbs. Cover and bring to the boil, then reduce the heat to a low simmer. Cook for 45 minutes, then turn off the heat. Leave to cool for 1 hour in the pot, then remove the chicken from the stockpot and allow the stock to reduce over a high heat until there is about 5cm (2 inches) of liquid left in the pan (about 600ml/20fl oz).

Meanwhile pick the chicken off the bones in bite-sized pieces and set aside, discarding the bones.

Melt the butter in a saucepan and whisk in the flour. Let it cook for 1 minute, then whisk in the cider and let it reduce by half. Strain, then whisk in the stock, bring to the boil, let the sauce thicken, then add the cream and Parmesan and season. Transfer to a mixing bowl and mix in the chicken.

Heat the oil in a frying pan and when it's hot fry the mushrooms for 1 minute. Add the garlic and some thyme leaves and season. Cook for a further minute, then add to the chicken mix and leave to cool.

Preheat the oven to 210°C/190°C fan (410°F), Gas Mark 6½. On a floured surface unroll each of the puff pastry sheets and roll out until they are both 3mm (⅛ inch) thick. Place on a baking sheet lined with parchment. Cover with clingfilm and chill for 15 minutes.

Cut out 2 pastry circles, 1 measuring 30cm (12 inches) in diameter and the other 35cm (14 inches). Place the smaller circle on the lined baking sheet, then layer the cold chicken mixture on top. Brush beaten egg around the outer edge, then cover with the larger pastry circle, pressing lightly to remove any trapped air. Select a bowl slightly larger than the dome of the pie and invert it over the pastry. Press down to seal. Scallop the edge and discard the pastry trimmings. Brush the top of the pastry with more beaten egg. With a paring knife, score a pinwheel pattern in the top, stopping short of the scalloped edge. Chill for 15 minutes, then bake for 45–50 minutes until golden and cooked through.

WHOLE BAKED SALMON
WITH BRIGHT GREEN PARSLEY SAUCE

* SERVES 8, OR 10 ALONGSIDE PLENTY OF SIDE DISHES
* PREPARATION TIME: 30 MINUTES
* COOKING TIME: 25 MINUTES

In most of Europe it's classic to eat fish on Christmas Eve. It's a tradition I was brought up with, probably because my mum is half Polish. Sadly we don't really do it any more – we've sort of taken an Italian feasting angle, but I intend to slowly bring it back in. This is a great recipe for the lazybones among us... Baking a whole side of salmon is so easy – it's fridge-to-table in about 40 minutes. It's a classic combo of flavours, using the much under-used velouté sauce technique. I'd serve this simply with some buttery new potatoes. A good tip: in order to keep the sauce's vibrant green colour, don't add the spinach and parsley until just before you need it.

1 side of fresh good-quality farmed salmon

50g (1¾oz) unsalted butter at room temperature

100ml (3½oz) white wine

2 bay leaves

sea salt flakes and freshly ground black pepper

For the parsley sauce

30g (1oz) unsalted butter

30g (1oz) plain flour

50ml (1¾oz) white wine

400ml (14 fl oz) fish or white chicken stock

100ml (3½fl oz) milk

2 handfuls of baby spinach leaves

1 large bunch of parsley, about 60g (2¼oz)

1 tablespoon capers (in vinegar), drained

juice of ½ lemon

Heat the oven to 240°C/220°C fan (475°F), Gas Mark 9. Lay the salmon in a large roasting tray. Rub with the butter, then pour over the white wine, season and top with the bay leaves. Seal the edges of the roasting tray well with foil. Pop the salmon into the hot oven on a low shelf and bake for 25 minutes. Don't peek – leave the salmon to rest in the foil, which will give it just the perfect opaqueness that you want. If you like your salmon more cooked, add 5 minutes to the cooking time.

To make the parsley sauce, melt the butter in a small pan. Tip in the flour and whisk together with the butter. Let this mixture (the roux) cook out for 1 minute, otherwise the sauce will taste floury. Add the wine and allow the alcohol to evaporate. Slowly add the stock and milk and whisk until combined. Bring to the boil, then cook at a strong simmer for 10 minutes, or until the sauce has thickened and become rich, like a thick double pouring cream or even a thin custard. Add the spinach, parsley and capers and cook for 2 minutes. Blitz in a high-powered blender until the sauce is smooth. Sieve if you want a really silky sauce. Season with salt, pepper and the lemon juice.

Serve the salmon in slices with the parsley sauce and buttery new potatoes.

 SERVES 6

 PREPARATION TIME: 25 MINUTES, PLUS MARINATING

 COOKING TIME: 15 MINUTES

SMOKE-ROASTED TREACLE-CURED SALMON
WITH POTATO, CUCUMBER & BUTTERMILK SALAD

I first made this dish for a barbecue feature when I was working for the *Sunday Times Magazine* as a columnist, but while racking my brains for cool ways of cooking a Christmas salmon for this book, I couldn't get the treacle cure out of my head. Curing your salmon will season it, give it stacks of flavour, firm it up and allow it to cook really easily. This time it's being cooked in a super-hot oven to the point where it may even smoke a bit, which will only add flavour to the fish. If you're feeling like having some fun, layer some wood chips on a baking tray and douse them with 2 tablespoons vegetable oil mixed with 3 tablespoons water. Place the tray in the bottom of the oven five minutes before adding the fish and they will add even more smoky flavour.

1 x 600g (1lb 5oz) side of salmon, skin on, pin-boned

100g (3½oz) fine salt

100g (3½oz) caster sugar

3 tablespoons black treacle

1 tablespoon toasted fennel seeds

1 tablespoon coriander seeds

vegetable oil

For the salad

800g (1lb 12oz) Jersey Royals or other new potatoes, cooked until they just about break up with a fork

2 small Middle Eastern cucumbers, peeled, halved, deseeded and thinly sliced into half-moons

100g (3½oz) cornichons, thinly sliced

150ml (5fl oz) buttermilk or soured cream

2 tablespoons mayonnaise

2 tablespoons soured cream

a good squeeze of lemon juice

a good handful of dill, roughly chopped

sea salt flakes and freshly ground black pepper

Lay the salmon skin side down in a roasting tray. Blitz the salt, sugar, treacle and spices in a blender, until they just come together. Don't overdo it, or the ingredients will start to melt and be hard to handle. Sprinkle this salt mixture on to the pink surface of the salmon, wrap the tray in clingfilm, and leave to marinate for 2 hours.

Preheat the oven to 260°C/240°C fan (500°F), Gas Mark 10 or as high as your oven will go. While the oven is heating up, put your warm potatoes into a salad bowl. Add the sliced cucumber and cornichons. In a separate bowl, mix together the buttermilk, mayonnaise, soured cream, lemon juice and dill with some seasoning. Dress the salad with this buttermilk dressing while the potatoes are still warm.

When the oven is scorching hot, wash the cure off the fish and dry. Liberally rub the skin with oil and season with salt. Place a large baking tray in the oven with a generous glug of oil to prevent the fish from sticking, and let it get hot. Lay the fish skin side down on the hot tray. You need to roast it for 15–20 minutes, to allow the skin to get really crisp and dark and the fish to cook to the perfect opaque middle. Immediately, with 2 fish slices and some help from someone else, slide the salmon fillet off the tray and on to a platter to rest for 5 minutes. Serve the potato salad alongside the fish. Great with a simple watercress salad.

SALMON EN CROUTE
WITH PRAWN BISQUE SAUCE

This is a simple version of a classic salmon en croute, but made more special by serving it with a prawn sauce. The sauce maybe makes up for the simplicity of the en croute, which is simply salmon wrapped in seasoned spinach and puff pastry. The sauce is similar to a proper bisque in that it's made from the shells of the prawns, stock veg and herbs, a good lug of brandy and fish stock that's reduced down to a really intense shellfish "jus" thickened with cream. This is unashamedly the brainchild of me and my manager, Kate, when we were raving on about how brilliant it would be to merge salmon en croute and a prawn vol-au-vent. The result is far more elegant and outlandishly delicious.

For the sauce

2 tablespoons olive oil

1 onion, chopped

2 carrots, chopped

2 sticks of celery, chopped

1 fennel bulb, chopped

3 garlic cloves, peeled and left whole

2 bay leaves

a few thyme sprigs

a few parsley stalks

1 tablespoon tomato purée

24 raw king prawns, shelled and butterflied, shells reserved

a good lug of brandy or Cognac

1½ litres (2¾ pints) fish stock

150–200ml (5–7fl oz) double cream, depending how rich you like it

lemon juice, to taste

Heat the oil in a large heavy-bottomed saucepan. Toss in the onions, carrots, celery, fennel, garlic and herbs and sauté really slowly for about 20 minutes. This process is really important, as it is where you will get most of the flavour for your sauce. You want the vegetables to sweat really slowly and get really soft before they start to caramelize a little. You want a little colour, but not too much.

Add the tomato purée and stir to coat all the vegetables. You need to cook the purée for 1 minute to get rid of its raw flavour. Whack the heat up, then add the prawn shells, but not the prawn meat. Sauté the shells until they have turned bright pink, then douse with the brandy and cover with the stock. You need the stock to come above the shells. Cook for 20 minutes on a slow boil.

Pour through a sieve, collecting the fragrant prawn stock. Squash the shells, particularly the heads, so they release all their juices. Transfer the strained stock to a frying pan and boil it gently to reduce until it's really started to thicken and become intense in flavour. This process will probably reduce the volume of liquid by about two-thirds. Whisk in the cream, bring back to the boil until combined and thickened, then finish with a squeeze of lemon juice to cut through the richness. Set aside the sauce while you cook the rest of the dish. (You can make this in the morning and finish it in the evening if you like. If you do this, refrigerate it until you're ready to use it.)

OK, so making the salmon en croute is pretty simple. First you need to cook your spinach. In a large lidded pan, heat the oil or butter. When it's hot, add all the spinach and cover with a lid. Leave to cook for 30 seconds, then remove the lid and give a good stir. Pop the lid back on and cook for another minute, or

For the salmon en croute

1 tablespoon olive or rapeseed oil,
  or unsalted butter

2 x 225g (8oz) packets of spinach,
  washed, trimmed and chopped

2 x 325g (11½oz) packets of ready-
  rolled all-butter puff pastry

plain flour, for dusting

a really good fresh grating of nutmeg

1 x 1kg (2lb 4oz) (approx.) side of
  salmon, skinned and trimmed

2 free-range egg yolks, beaten

sea salt flakes and freshly ground
  black pepper

until the spinach is wilted down. Drain through a sieve, then run under cold water until chilled. Now you need to dry the spinach really well. I place it between loads of sheets of kitchen paper and squeeze out the water. It may take a few goes...

Unroll your sheets of puff pastry on a floured surface and roll them again with a floured rolling pin so that they are just bigger than the size of your salmon. Spread half the spinach over one pastry sheet, roughly the same size as your fish. Season the spinach with plenty of salt and pepper and a really good grating of nutmeg. Lay the salmon on top and cover with the rest of the spinach. Brush the edges of the pastry with some of the beaten egg, then lay the second layer of pastry over the top. Press the edges together to join the 2 sheets of pastry, then trim them, saving the trimmings for decoration. Now prick the top all over with a fork so that the pastry doesn't burst while cooking.

Roll out the pastry trimmings and cut into Christmassy shapes – I love stars or holly leaf shapes. Brush the top of the pastry all over with beaten egg to glaze, then stick the pastry decorations all over, however you like. Glaze them with the beaten egg, then pop on a baking tray, then into the fridge for 30 minutes to rest. I always add a final glaze before baking.

Meanwhile, heat the oven to 200°C/180°C fan (400°F), Gas Mark 6. Remove the salmon en croute from the fridge and bake for 30–35 minutes, or until the pastry is golden brown and cooked through. The pastry and the salmon cook at pretty much exactly the same time.

Finish the sauce by frying the prawns quickly in butter in a frying pan, over a fierce heat, until tinged brown on each side but still raw in the middle. Pour the sauce over the prawns, then reduce the temperature and simmer until piping hot and the prawns are cooked through. Serve the salmon en croute cut into slices, with the prawn sauce alongside.

CORIANDER, CHILLI & LIME-CURED SALMON
WITH AVOCADO SALAD

The most popular starter for Christmas Day is still smoked salmon. I totally understand that. It's what I usually have too. But smoked salmon is not always what it appears – some are made with sulphates – and with more of us interested in what's in our food, it's good to cure our own. Now, if you have an indoor smoker this is a really great way to cure your fish before you smoke it, but this cure is so flavourful you don't need to. I'm making this like the Swedes do and curing it like gravlax, but with Mexican flavours. It's really easy, and makes a terrific starter with the avocado salad, or a light lunch after all the gluttony. (See photograph on pages 136–7.)

1 whole side of salmon (about 900g/2lb), skinned and pin-boned (ask your fishmonger to do this)

1 large bunch of coriander, roughly chopped

2 green chillies

1 tablespoon black pepper

1 teaspoon coriander seeds

finely grated zest of 4 limes (reserve the juice for the dressing), plus extra lime wedges to serve

50ml tequila

150g (5½oz) caster sugar

130g (4¾oz) fine salt

For the salad

½ garlic clove, crushed

1 tablespoon lime juice

2 tablespoons olive oil

2 ripe avocados, chopped

2 radishes, finely sliced

2 spring onions, finely sliced

1 red or green chilli, finely chopped

a handful of fresh coriander, chopped

Lay the salmon on a large roasting tray or flat dish. Put the rest of the curing ingredients into a food processor and blitz until smooth. Rub the marinade all over the fish, then wrap in clingfilm and place in the fridge. After 12 hours, wipe off the marinade and pop the salmon back into the fridge for a minimum of overnight, or up to 24 hours.

The next day, make the dressing for the salad: mix together the garlic, lime juice and oil. In a separate bowl, mix together the avocados, radishes, spring onions, chilli and coriander, then stir in the dressing.

Slice the cured salmon thinly and lay about 6–8 slices on each plate. Serve with lime wedges and a few tablespoons of the avocado salad.

BUTTERY WHOLE BAKED HADDOCK
WITH WOODY HERBS

This is about as classic as it gets for Christmas Eve. So many nationalities bake a whole fish – the Italians and Spanish would opt for a whole sea fish, such as hake or bass, while the Eastern Europeans might choose a river fish such as pike, or a whole cod. The wealthy may go for a turbot which is one of the finest fish in the sea, but when I was a nipper we didn't have that kind of cash, so my mum would bake a whole haddock, with woody herbs, butter and a splash of wine and lemon. I think it's easiest to steam-bake it, by wrapping it in foil. It makes it foolproof, whereas roasting can make it dry out. I would serve this with new potatoes that have been boiled or salt-boiled (see page 116), or even mash, and some greens.

150g (5½oz) unsalted butter,
 at room temperature

1 whole haddock (about 1.5–2kg
 (3–4½lb) scaled and gutted with
 the head left on (it gives stacks of
 flavour to the sauce)

4 bay leaves

a good few rosemary sprigs

a good few lemon thyme
 (or thyme) sprigs

100ml (3½fl oz) dry white wine

a squeeze of lemon juice

sea salt flakes and freshly ground
 black pepper

This is really simple. Start off by heating the oven to 240°C/ 220°C fan (475°F), Gas Mark 9. Lay out 2 sheets of foil twice the size of the fish on the kitchen counter, one on top of the other. Rub 40g (1½oz) of the butter over the centre part of the foil. Place the fish in the middle of the foil, then rub the rest of the butter all over it, inside the cavity and out, and season it liberally all over. Stuff the fish with the herbs and douse it with the white wine and lemon juice.

Enclose the foil around the fish, leaving a little space around it for it to steam, and crimp the edges together tightly so that no air can escape. Pop the foil parcel on a baking tray and bake for 35 minutes for perfect opaque fish. As the fish cooks, the butter will melt and create a fantastic sauce with the fish juices and wine.

Open the parcel and carefully transfer the fish on to a serving dish. If the sauce is too watery, pour it into a small saucepan, bring to the boil and allow it to reduce until it's thickened and full of flavour. Season with more salt and pepper if you need it, and maybe even a spot more lemon juice. Serve the fish with the sauce.

Three fantastic wreaths

Here are three ideas to create homemade festive wreaths. You can buy wire, natural rattan or polystyrene wreath frames online or from craft stores such as Hobbycraft.

HERB WREATH

You will need:

florist's wire

1 x wire or natural rattan wreath frame, about 40cm (16 inches)

5 bunches of fresh rosemary

a good handful of medium-sized elastic bands

wire cutters

5 bunches of fresh thyme

5 bunches of fresh sage

2 bunches bay leaves

Wrap florist's wire around the wreath frame in a criss-cross pattern at intervals of about 2cm (¾ inch) – this is to attach the herbs to.

Divide the rosemary into bunches of 5–7 stems and bind the stalks of each bunch with elastic bands.

Secure the first bunch to the frame using wire, wrapping it around the stalks and cutting any excess with wire cutters. Place the next bundle of herbs so that the leaves cover the stems of the previous bunch – you only want the leaves on show. Continue this process until one-quarter of the frame is covered in the first herb. Repeat with the remaining 3 herbs until the frame is covered.

CRANBERRY WREATH

You will need:

cocktail sticks

approx 2kg (4lb 8oz) fresh cranberries

1 x styrofoam or polystyrene wreath ring (as big as you like but with at least 5cm/2 inches width)

2m (6½ft) wide ribbon

Break the cocktail sticks in half. Take one half stick and poke the broken end into the base of each cranberry. Then simply stick each cranberry into the Styrofoam – I like to do this in concentric circles to create a uniform pattern.

Continue this process until the base is entirely covered, then add a ribbon to finish. This wreath should last at least a week, especially if it's cold outside!

POM-POM WREATH

You will need:

glue gun

1 x styrofoam or polystyrene wreath ring (as big as you like but with at least 5cm/2 inches width)

pom-poms, in various colours and sizes

Using the glue gun, simply cover the base with pom-poms. I find it easier to stick the big ones on first and then fill in the gaps with smaller ones.

SAGE, PARMESAN & LEMON VEAL MILANESE
WITH TOMATO SPAGHETTI

My sisters and I were brought up on veal Milanese (breaded veal), eaten the Anglo-Italian way, with spaghetti and tomato sauce. The spaghetti sauce is made sweeter and fresher by using canned cherry tomatoes (a terrific store-cupboard ingredient). I've breaded the veal with extra-crispy panko breadcrumbs flavoured with sage, lemon and Parmesan, which gives it an extra flavour whack. Eating this on Christmas Eve every year has become, I guess, a really random tradition, and while now when we entertain we serve it in a more Italian style, at the same time as a whole fish for example, I appreciate it's probably still a bit crazy – but then, that's my family for you and it would have been weird not to have included it here. So... this one's for you, Munds and Bubs! The classic weird Erskine – for no reason whatsoever except that we all love it – a Christmas Eve spesh.

100g (3½oz) panko or fresh white breadcrumbs

20 fresh sage leaves, very finely chopped

finely grated zest of 2 lemons (keep the lemons for the wedges)

50g (1¾oz) Parmesan cheese, finely grated, plus extra to serve

4 x 150g (5½oz) veal escalopes (go for British rose veal if you can find it – better conditions, happier cows – or, if you still feel funny about veal, which you shouldn't as its part of the dairy trade, bash out some pork chops or chicken breasts)

100g (3½oz) plain flour

1 large free-range egg, lightly beaten

100ml (3½fl oz) olive oil

lemon wedges, to serve

sea salt flakes and freshly ground black pepper

Mix together the panko crumbs, sage, lemon zest and Parmesan. Lay the veal escalopes on a chopping board and cover each one with a couple of sheets of clingfilm. Using a meat tenderizer or a rolling pin, bash each escalope until it is about 2–3mm (about ⅛ inch) thick.

Season the flour with salt and pepper, then put the flour, egg and breadcrumbs into separate bowls. Dip each escalope first into the flour, then coat with the beaten egg and finally with the breadcrumbs. Put the crumbed escalopes into the fridge to chill while you make the spaghetti sauce.

For the sauce, heat the 1 tablespoon of oil in a small pan. Throw in the onion and cook over a low heat for around 8 minutes, or until softened. For the last minute of cooking, add the garlic. Add the canned tomatoes to the pan along with the tomato purée, sugar, vinegar, and the basil, torn into pieces. Season with salt and pepper and leave to bubble away for 20 minutes. Halfway through, get the spaghetti cooking in plenty of salted boiling water.

For the cherry tomato & basil spaghetti

1 tablespoon olive oil

1 small onion, peeled and finely chopped

3 garlic cloves, peeled and finely chopped

2 x 400g (14oz) cans of cherry tomatoes

1 tablespoon tomato purée

1 tablespoon golden caster sugar

a splash of sherry vinegar or red wine
    vinegar

a small bunch of fresh basil leaves

350g (12oz) spaghetti

sea salt flakes and freshly ground
    black pepper

Once the spaghetti is on, heat the 100ml (3½fl oz) of oil in a frying pan. Lay the breaded escalopes in the oil carefully (if they are very large you may need to cook them in batches). Fry the escalopes for 3 minutes on each side, depending on how thick they are, until the breadcrumbs are golden brown.

Drain the escalopes on kitchen paper. Drain the spaghetti and mix with the cherry tomato sauce. Serve the spaghetti with the veal, some lemon wedges and a decent shaving of Parmesan cheese.

Like most winter celebrations, many of the Christian Christmas traditions we know today have ancient, pre-Christian origins, that often focused on nature. The date of December 25th wasn't fixed by the Christian church until 440AD, but the timing coincided with the winter solstice. During the pre-Christmas Roman festival of Saturnalia, houses would be decorated with evergreens, to honour Saturn, the god of agriculture, in the hope he would bless the crops in the following spring. Spherical decorations, to represent the sun and fruits of the earth were hung on these branches, which are a likely predecessor for our modern day baubles. The Druids believed that mistletoe could cure illness, promote fertility and protect against witchcraft. This, combined with the belief in Norse mythology that mistletoe was a sign of love, is probably where our habit of sneaking a cheeky kiss underneath a few hanging sprigs stems from. Holly and ivy have long held potent symbolism. As well as everlasting life, holly came to represent Christ's crown of thorns; the berries, his blood. Ivy was hoped to protect the household against drunkenness. (I for one will be getting it in by the armful for next year in that case!)

Most households in the UK will roast a turkey for their main meal on Christmas Day. Turkey was brought to these shores from the New World by trader William Strickland in 1526. He sold the birds at Bristol port for tuppence each. Ever since they have grown in popularity, partly due to the fact turkeys are quick to fatten. King Henry VIII is reportedly the first English monarch to enjoy a slice of turkey at his Christmas feast, but you were more likely to find wild boar, goose or capon pre-16th century, (or even swan and peacock if you were really posh). I've included two recipes for turkey and goose as I would be delighted with either on Christmas Day.

No matter where you are in the world, you will always find some kind of cake or pudding on the Christmas table, whether that is a fruity, zesty cheesecake in Poland, a *buche de noel* in France, or a panettone in Italy. In Britain, Christmas pudding is an iconic mainstay of the Yuletide table, dating back to medieval times. Before the 19th century it was called "plum pudding" (where "plums" actually referred to raisins). Old recipes often have 13 ingredients, thought to represent Christ and his 12 apostles. It was traditionally made on or directly after the "Sunday next before Advent" – this later became known as "stir-up Sunday" when everyone in the household, especially any children, would give the mixture a stir while making a wish. Conventionally the pudding mixture would be stirred in the direction of East to West to honour the journey made by the Three Wise Men in the story of the Nativity. It is still common to stir a lucky coin into the mixture, but in the past this extended to a small wishbone for good fortune, a thimble to represent thriftiness, or even a miniature anchor to symbolize safe harbour. I've tried lots of Christmas pudding recipes over the years, and I think I've now finally found "the one" – see my recipe for The Best Christmas Pudding in the World!

To help you take away the stress and pressure of preparing your Christmas feast I've also included in this chapter a handy Christmas countdown to the big day.

Christmas
Day

Christmas Countdown!

I'm not going to pretend that organization is my strong suit, BUT avoiding stress is the key to enjoying the festive period – the idea is to have a good time, not a nervous breakdown. Recipes for my Christmas puddings, mincemeat, chutneys and Christmas cake will improve greatly with a bit of maturing time, so if you can make any of these in advance it will make your life easier. With a bit of forward planning things will go a whole lot smoother, so here is a breakdown of steps for the weeks leading up to Christmas, and for the day itself.

3 MONTHS BEFORE:

Make your Christmas puddings and leave them somewhere cool and dry to mature.

2 MONTHS BEFORE:

Make your mincemeat, chutneys and Christmas cake.

1 MONTH BEFORE:

Order your turkey or goose, ham or any other large roasting joints, sausagemeat and fresh meat stocks. If possible, patronize local butchers or farm shops, or place your order online. My favourites are www.copasturkeys. co.uk and www.turnerandgeorge.co.uk.

1 WEEK BEFORE:

Buy all your other ingredients, such as fruit and vegetables, alcohol, cheese and so on. Be methodical and read through all the recipes you are intending to cook and write a detailed shopping list so you don't forget anything. I find this really helpful to avoid buying too much and over-spending. Again, I think it's so important to support your local grocer, fishmonger, wine merchant and delis wherever possible.

CHRISTMAS EVE:

Brine the turkey or goose. Don't forget to take out the giblets and keep them in the fridge for the gravy. You can also make your gravy stock the night before if you wish.

Prepare A Wreath of Pigs in Blankets (see page 196) and your choice of stuffings (see pages 167–9 and 172) and leave in the fridge overnight.

Braised Sour Red Cabbage (see page 185) can be made the night before and heated up on Christmas day.

If you're making the Clementine & Ginger Trifle (see page 198) this can also be prepared today.

Make any starters or desserts that need overnight setting in the fridge, such as The Creamiest & Lightest Christmas Chicken Liver Parfait (see page 108). Recipes such as the Baked Jerusalem Artichoke, Spinach & Parmesan Dip (see page 58) or Brown Shrimp Gratin (see page 61) can be can be made in advance and left in the fridge overnight.

CHRISTMAS DAY:

Obviously these timings are open to interpretation, depending on what time you wish to eat and the weight of your turkey. In my family we like to eat at 3ish.

✳ **9am:**
Remove the turkey or goose from the brine and allow it to come up to room temperature.

✳ **10am:**
Preheat the oven for the turkey.

Prepare the turkey or goose for the oven (see pages 158, 160 or 164), stuffing it if you are using (see page 173). Make sure you have calculated the right weight and cooking time.

✳ **10.30am:**
Get the turkey in the oven! Set your oven timer! Don't forget to leave time for the turkey to rest, as this will also free up oven space for your potatoes, carrots and parsnips.

For Perfect Roast Potatoes, peel, chop and parboil your potatoes. You want them to steam as dry as possible before roasting (see page 179). Set aside.

Trim Brussels sprouts and set aside in a bowl of cold water.

✳ **11am:**
Prepare the Really Simple Honey Glazed Carrots & Parsnips in the tin you are roasting them in (see page 186).

The same for the Sprouts, Smoked Bacon & Chestnuts (see page 190).

✳ **12pm:**
Lay the table (see pages 170–1).
Have a glass of something with alcohol in it. And a little sit down.

✳ **12.45pm:**
Prepare the Cranberry, Port & Clementine Sauce (see page 194) and the Gingerbread Sauce (see page 195). You can reheat the sauces just before you are ready to eat.

✳ **1.45pm:**
Put your potatoes in the oven to roast.

Make the stock for The Best Christmas Gravy (see page 159), if you didn't last night.

✳ **2.00pm:**
Remove the turkey from the oven and leave to rest covered in foil.

✳ **2.15pm:**
Cook your sprouts.

Turn the potatoes over and put back in the oven Put the carrots and parsnips in the oven to roast.

✳ **2.30pm:**
Put your Wreath of Pigs in Blankets in the oven to cook.

✳ **2.45pm:**
Put plates in the oven to warm up if you have space.

Finish the gravy (see page 159).

Reheat any prepared red cabbage and sauces.

✳ **3.00pm:**
SERVE!

CHARRED BLOOD ORANGE MIMOSA

By charring the oranges you get a more caramelized flavour to the juice, taking the everyday mimosa (OK, maybe not every day) to the next level.

6 ripe blood oranges

small knob of unsalted butter

1 teaspoon caster sugar (optional)

1 bottle of medium-dry prosecco

Preheat the oven to 200°C/180°C fan (400°F), Gas Mark 6.

Cut the oranges in half. Put the butter into a large frying pan and get it really hot. Place the oranges flat sides down in the pan and leave to char for 5–10 minutes. You want to get them nice and black. Once this is done, put the oranges into a roasting tray and roast for about 20 minutes. Remove from the oven and leave to cool.

Squeeze the juice from the oranges. Blood oranges can be a little bitter at the beginning of the season, so make sure you give the juice a little taste. You might want to add the 1 teaspoon of sugar if this is the case.

Half-fill your champagne flutes with juice (approximately 75ml/2½fl oz per glass) and top up with chilled prosecco. Serve immediately.

CHOCOLATE-ORANGE CREAM LIQUEUR

Christmas without a Terry's Chocolate Orange just isn't Christmas. Christmas isn't Christmas without some cream liqueur over ice. I'VE MERGED THEM INTO ONE. Making your own knocks spots off the shop-bought stuff. It's utter filth! Makes a great gift, too (see photograph on page 152).

100g (3½oz) milk chocolate

100g (3½oz) dark chocolate

300ml (10fl oz) whole milk

2 free-range egg yolks

150ml (5fl oz) double cream

1 x 410g (14½oz) can of condensed milk

a pinch of sea salt flakes

finely grated zest of 3 clementines or 1 orange

350ml (12fl oz) good-quality vodka

ice cubes, to serve

Melt the chocolate in a few tablespoons of the milk in a saucepan over a low heat, stirring regularly. Next, add the egg yolks and whisk continuously, to create a custard rather than scrambled egg! Stir in the remaining milk, cream, condensed milk, salt and clementine zest. Pour through a sieve into a large bowl. Cover the surface directly with clingfilm and leave to cool. The clingfilm helps prevent a nasty skin forming on the top.

Once the mixture is at room temperature, add the vodka and stir in well. Pour into sterilized bottles. I like to keep it in the fridge. It keeps for about 10 days. Serve in a coupe over lots of ice.

MELLOW YELLOW
BLOODY 'ELL ROSIE

This is my mate Rose's drink. It's pretty much a classic Bloody Mary, but made with gin and yellow tomato juice and with English mustard replacing the horseradish. Yellow tomato juice is much sweeter – it's odd, it almost has a peachy tang to it. It seems unfair to call it a "Bloody" Mary so I renamed it, after Rose herself!

50g (1¾oz) crushed sea salt flakes mixed with 1 teaspoon freshly ground black pepper, to rim the glass with

850ml (1½ pints) yellow tomato juice

200ml (7fl oz) gin

2 teaspoons Tabasco sauce

2 teaspoons celery salt

2 tablespoons Worcestershire sauce

2 tablespoons lemon juice

3 teaspoons English mustard

sea salt flakes and lots of freshly ground pepper

To serve

ice cubes

celery sticks, green olives and cherry tomatoes

First prep your glasses: take 4 highball glasses or tumblers, dip the rims in water, then dip them in the salt and pepper mixture.

Mix all your ingredients in a large jug, making sure the mustard is well mixed in (I like to use a sauce whisk). Fill your glasses with plenty of ice cubes and pour over the mix. Pop a celery stick and the rest of the garnishes into each glass and get drinking.

BRILLIANT WET-BRINED SPICED TURKEY

Nigella Lawson made the brined turkey a thing when she released her book *Feast*. It was as if she'd turned everything we know about Christmas on its head. Brining (or reverse osmosis, if you want to be technical) works simply because the salt draws out the excess water from the meat, also compacting the meat to the bone. What it leaves is a firm, juicy, easy-to-carve bird that's infused with all the flavours you've brined it in. I am eternally grateful to Nigella for this, because it was the first time I had seen anyone brining poultry on a domestic level. In restaurants we've been brining for yonks, and many of the poultry dishes I'm known for (my Korean wings) are brined. Try it – it's a revelation. I use a mega industrial stockpot to brine my turkey, but most homes won't have one of these and it's perfectly acceptable to use a clean bin or large plastic storage box. So here's my own recipe – I hope you try it and it changes your life, just like Nigella's did mine...

For the brine

500g (1lb 2oz) fine salt

150g (5½oz) maple syrup or brown sugar

1 free-range Kelly Bronze turkey (I think Copas are the best turkeys on the block), about 4kg (8lb 12oz), giblets removed for the gravy

5 mandarins, cut in half widthways

2 lemons, sliced

12 cloves

12 allspice berries

5 star anise

2 cinnamon sticks

10 peppercorns

2 bay leaves

3 rosemary sprigs

5–6 thyme sprigs

a small bunch of parsley

4 onions, sliced

1 garlic bulb, cut in half crossways

50g (1¾oz) unsalted butter

sea salt flakes, for sprinkling

Heat 1 litre (1¾ pints) of water in a pan on the stove, then pour in the salt and syrup or sugar and allow to dissolve – this is the beginning of your brine. Place the turkey in your brining vessel and cover with cold water, then pour over the salt and sugar solution. Add the mandarins, lemon slices, spices, herbs, 2 of the sliced onions and the garlic bulb. Cover and place in the fridge if it'll fit, or somewhere cold in the house or garden if not (if it's the garden, make sure it's VERY secure so the foxes or cats can't get it... can you imagine?) and leave overnight.

Next day, remove the turkey from the brine and let it come to room temperature about an hour before cooking.

Preheat the oven to 200°C/180°C fan (400°F), Gas Mark 6. Pat the turkey dry with kitchen paper, then rub it all over with butter. Carefully slide your hand under the skin to detach it from the breast, just enough to rub the butter underneath. Sprinkle the bird with sea salt flakes.

Put the remaining sliced onions in the bottom of a large roasting tray to act as a trivet for the bird. Sit the turkey on top and cover completely with foil, tucking it under the tray to create a foil tent. Cook the turkey for 25 minutes per kilo (1 hour 40 minutes for a 4kg/8lb 12oz bird), making that 35 minutes per kilo if you have stuffed the bird. Take out the turkey and increase the oven temperature to 240°C/220°C fan (475°F), Gas Mark 9.

For the best Christmas gravy

the neck and gizzard from the giblets

1 onion, sliced

1 carrot, sliced

1 bay leaf

1.2 litres (2 pints) fresh chicken stock
   or cold water

2 tablespoons plain flour

1 large (I'll let you be the judge of that)
   glass of white wine

sea salt flakes and freshly ground
   black pepper

Remove the foil and return the turkey to the oven until golden – about 30 minutes. To test, pierce the fattest part of the thigh with a skewer. The juices should run clear. Rest the turkey, covered loosely with foil, for at least 30 minutes and up to 1 hour before serving (strain the cooking juices and keep the onions to use in the gravy).

The best Christmas gravy

To make the gravy, make a simple stock from the neck and gizzard: place them in a small pan with the onion, carrot and bay leaf. Cover with fresh chicken stock or cold water and simmer for 1 hour. Strain and set aside.

Pour out any juices from the roasting tray while your turkey is resting. Stir the flour into the roasting tray with the onions leftover from cooking the turkey, place over a highish heat cook the flour for 1 minute, scraping away at the meaty sediment at the bottom of the pan. Pour over the white wine, let it bubble away until the pan starts to hiss again, then pour over the strained stock, whisking as you go. Let the gravy bubble away gently until it becomes reduced, rich and full of flavour. Season to taste and serve piping hot.

SPICED DRY-BRINED TURKEY

One of my best chef friends is the barbeque whizz-kid Neil Rankin. Neil is renowned for how he cooks meat, having been head chef at the world-famous Pitt Cue Co. restaurant, and now runs a series of places from his own restaurant Smokehouse to being the "food boss" at Street Feast in London. We fight all the time about brining. He is a master at what he does, and after having wet-brined for what seems like forever, he now sees more value in going dry, as he feels that the additional water seeps into the meat, adds false moisture, and takes out concentrated flavour. We now know dry-brined bacon cooks and tastes better than wet-brined. I still believe that by being immersed in a wet solution, the power of osmosis from the salt solution draws out the excess moisture and leaves the meat more firmly compacted to the bone AND makes it easier to cook. With guaranteed juiciness, the brine acts similarly to a marinade and takes advantage of all the flavours. Here is what we can agree on: if you dry-brine, you need to brine for much longer (24–48 hours), cook the meat MUCH slower, at a rather staggering 140°C/120°C fan (275°F) Gas Mark 1 (with a quick spike at the end for golden skin). I'll give it to him, it does make a delicious turkey, BUT to get the same juiciness (albeit a more forced juiciness with the wet brine), it's a slightly more technical process and perhaps not one for the inexperienced home cook. For the more adventurous cooks – do try this recipe. (See photograph on page 157).

1 free-range Kelly Bronze turkey, about 4–5kg (10–11lb), giblets removed for the gravy

12 cloves

12 allspice berries

5 star anise

2 cinnamon sticks

10 peppercorns

500g (1lb 2oz) fine salt

150g (5½oz) brown sugar

2 bay leaves

3 rosemary sprigs

5–6 thyme sprigs

finely grated zest of 2 mandarins

finely grated zest of 2 lemons

50g (1¾ oz) unsalted butter

20 streaky bacon rashers

2 onions, sliced

The Best Christmas Gravy, to serve (see page 159)

You can get these brilliant turkey brining bags (I get mine from Lakeland, www.lakeland.co.uk). Pop your turkey into the bag and crack on with the dry brine. Place the cloves, allspice, star anise, cinnamon and peppercorns in a pan and toast them for 2–3 minutes. Place in a blender with the salt, sugar, herbs and zest and blitz until you have a spiced salt. Pour the salt into the brining bag with the turkey and give it a good old shake until the turkey is covered inside AND out with the mixture. Pop it into the fridge and leave for up to 48 hours.

When ready to cook, heat the oven to 140°C/120°C fan (275°F) Gas Mark 1. This sounds alarmingly low. Trust me, I was alarmed when Neil told me, but go with it, it works. You now need to wash off the salt mixture and dry the bird really well. Carefully slide your hand under the skin to detach it from the breast, just enough to rub the butter underneath. Do your best to rub it evenly under the skin, but if there's any excess butter you can rub it over the top of the bird. No need to season, as the bird has been brined.

If you're stuffing your bird, now's the time! I do, because I like the meat juices to make my stuffing moist with the added flavour from the bird.

Next lay the bacon over the breast of the bird. You can get all fancy pants and make a lattice shape if you like, but this bacon is just to keep the breast moist and for more flavour.

Lay the bird on a trivet of the sliced onions in a large roasting tray and wrap tightly in foil. Roast for 3½ hours – there really is no need to baste when cooking at so low a temperature, so don't remove the foil. It kind of roasts/steams the bird, which is how it keeps it juicy. When the time is up, take the bird out of the oven and increase the oven temperature as high as it will go. Remove the foil while the oven heats up and check that the bird is cooked by piercing the thigh at its thickest part with a metal skewer. The juices should run clear and it should be really juicy. Roast for another 20 minutes, or until the bird is an even bronze colour all over. Remove from the oven and wrap in fresh foil, then leave to rest for 40 minutes before serving with The Best Christmas Gravy.

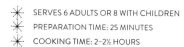

* SERVES 6 ADULTS OR 8 WITH CHILDREN
* PREPARATION TIME: 25 MINUTES
* COOKING TIME: 2–2½ HOURS

ROAST GOOSE
WITH CHESTNUT, APPLE & PRUNE STUFFING

I wish I was allowed to eat goose on Christmas Day but my family have vetoed it, so I make sure I cook it in the run-up to Christmas. I've played around with so many different recipes, but the best way is to use the Chinese crispy duck technique to ensure really crisp thin skin and pink breast meat. This involves drenching it with ROASTING hot liquor that's infused with Asian flavours (which incidentally transfer brilliantly as Christmas flavours). You then need to dry it overnight until the skin goes really waxy. This is the best goose recipe I've tried, and the gravy is a winner, starring equally with a Chestnut, Apple & Prune stuffing on the plate (see page 176). See photograph on page 163. I would serve this with Roasted Black Grapes (see opposite), and for a Christmas feast serve with Gingerbread Sauce (see page 195), A Wreath of Pigs in Blankets (see page 196) and use the goose fat for the potatoes (see page 179).

5 litres (9 pints) water

3 star anise

2 cinnamon sticks

5 slices of fresh root ginger, bruised

2 spring onions, split down the middle

5 tablespoons maltose (if you really can't find it, use honey)

4 tablespoons light soy sauce

2 tablespoons sea salt flakes

1 x 5kg (11lb) free-range goose, cleaned of its offal and excess fat

1 x recipe Chestnut, Apple & Prune Stuffing (see page 176)

For the gravy

the goose's neck and gizzards (if available)

1 onion, sliced

1 tablespoon plain flour

100ml (3½fl oz) port

1 bay leaf

500ml (18fl oz) fresh chicken stock

Place the water, star anise, cinnamon, ginger, spring onions, maltose, soy and salt in a pan and bring to the boil. Turn off the heat and leave to infuse for 10 minutes. Prick the goose all over with a tiny needle. This takes quite a bit of time, but it's worth it for really crispy skin, as it allows the fat to pour out of it. Place the goose in the sink and pour the boiling hot infused stock all over it (discard the stock afterwards). The idea is that the skin will tighten up. Now place on a wire rack and leave in the fridge to dry for 15 hours. The skin of the goose will feel like wax paper when it's dry.

Now stuff the bird with your Chestnut, Apple & Prune Stuffing, then you need to weigh it.

Preheat the oven to 240°C/220°C fan (475°F), Gas Mark 9. Place a trivet or rack in a roasting tin and place the goose on top. Roast for 15 minutes, then reduce the oven temperature to 200°C/180°C fan (400°F), Gas Mark 6 and cook for 20 minutes per kilo for medium-rare, 30 minutes per kilo for well-done.

Remove the bird from the oven and leave to rest for 30 minutes. It's worth noting that the goose will leak tons of its fat, which is terrific to keep for roasting your potatoes, but keep an eye on it and pour away the fat as you see fit.

When the goose is resting out of the roasting tray, remove the rack or trivet if you used one and place the roasting tray on the hob over a low-ish heat. Chop the goose neck into 4 through the joint and brown the pieces in the tray with the gizzards. Add the onion and cook for 4 minutes, or until a little soft and golden. Now add the flour and scrape away at the bottom of the pan to lift up all the meaty bits and goosey juices. Pour in the port and whisk like crazy. It will fast become a purple gunge. Now add the bay leaf and pour in the stock slowly, whisking as you go, until combined. Now bring the gravy to the boil and reduce until the flavour is right and it's a good pouring consistency.

Serve the goose with the gravy poured over.

ROASTED BLACK GRAPES

SERVES 6–8
PREPARATION TIME: 5 MINUTES
COOKING TIME: 15–20 MINUTES

By simply roasting black grapes alongside your goose, you get the same sort of concentrated sweet and tangy flavour as you would from an apple sauce or anything else you would normally accompany goose or duck with, but it's way easier, looks stunning, and a grape has the right balance of sweetness and acidity to sit alongside said goose and the rest of the trimmings!

300g (10½oz) black seedless grapes
1 tablespoon olive oil
¼ teaspoon sea salt flakes

Preheat the oven to 220°C/200°C fan (425°F), Gas Mark 7.

Once the oven is hot, place the grapes on a roasting tray, drizzle over the oil and sprinkle them with a little salt. Place in the oven for 15 minutes, until the grapes start to blister and caramelize on the outside, and become soft and intense inside.

THREE GREAT SAUSAGEMEAT STUFFINGS FOR TURKEY OR CHICKEN

OK, so I've tested all kinds of stuffings while working on this book and I can't help but feel that while other stuffings are nice, they don't come close to a really good sausagemeat stuffing. Without sausagemeat they seem to be a little empty. The whole thing is umami-ed up to the eyeballs and I just love that kind of flavour. All these stuffings will fill a turkey cavity perfectly, or a capon, rooster or goose with a little overspill that you can shape into balls and wrap with thinly sliced smoked streaky bacon, to serve alongside. So they will all (at a squeeze) serve up to 10 people.

 PREPARATION TIME: 20 MINUTES
COOKING TIME: 15 MINUTES,
PLUS COOKING TIME OF BIRD

PROPER SAGE & ONION STUFFING

1 tablespoon olive oil

4 onions, finely chopped

3 garlic cloves, finely chopped

a few thyme sprigs

1–2 rosemary sprigs, leaves picked
and chopped

450g (1lb) sausagemeat

the bird's offal (liver and kidneys),
roughly chopped (optional)

100g (3½oz) fresh white breadcrumbs

a small bunch of sage leaves,
thinly sliced

finely grated zest of 1 lemon

a large pinch of freshly grated nutmeg

sea salt flakes and freshly ground
black pepper

Heat the oil in a frying pan. Add the onions and fry very slowly over a low-ish heat for 20–25 minutes, or until they have softened and are tinged golden. For the last minute of cooking, add the garlic, thyme and rosemary.

Remove from the heat and put into a mixing bowl with the sausagemeat, offal, breadcrumbs, sage, lemon zest, nutmeg and a good sprinkling of salt and pepper. Roll up your sleeves and get squelching it together, really giving it a good mix to make sure it's combined. Put in a bowl and keep it in the fridge until you are ready to use it (see page 173).

PROPER CHESTNUT STUFFING

1 tablespoon olive oil

200g (7oz) good-quality smoked streaky bacon, finely chopped

2 onions, finely chopped

3 garlic cloves, finely chopped

a few thyme sprigs, leaves picked

450g (1lb) sausagemeat

the bird's offal (liver and kidneys), roughly chopped (optional)

100g (3½oz) fresh white breadcrumbs

a small bunch of parsley, chopped

finely grated zest of 1 lemon

a large pinch of freshly grated nutmeg

200g (7oz) peeled vacuum-packed chestnuts, chopped

sea salt flakes and freshly ground black pepper

Heat the oil in a frying pan. Add the bacon and fry for 5 minutes, until turning slightly golden. Add the onions and fry over a lowish heat for 8 minutes, or until they have begun to soften. For the last minute of cooking, add the garlic and thyme.

Remove from the heat and put into a mixing bowl with the sausagemeat, offal, breadcrumbs, parsley, lemon zest, nutmeg, chestnuts and a good sprinkling of salt and pepper. Roll up your sleeves and get squelching it together, really giving it a good mix to make sure it's combined. Put in a bowl and keep it in the fridge until you are ready to use it (see page 173).

JEWELLED FRUIT & NUT STUFFING

1 tablespoon olive oil

200g (7oz) good-quality smoked streaky bacon, finely chopped

2 onions, finely chopped

3 garlic cloves, finely chopped

a few thyme sprigs, leaves picked

1–2 rosemary sprigs, and finely chopped

450g (1lb) sausagemeat

the bird's offal (liver and kidneys), roughly chopped (optional)

100g (3½oz) fresh white breadcrumbs

a small bunch of parsley, chopped

finely grated zest of 1 lemon

finely grated zest of 1 orange

a large pinch of freshly grated nutmeg

200g (7oz) peeled vacuum-packed chestnuts, chopped

70g (2½oz) dried ready-to-eat apricots, chopped

70g (2½oz) dried cranberries

70g (2½oz) pistachio nuts

sea salt flakes and freshly ground black pepper

Heat the oil in a frying pan. Add the bacon and fry for 5 minutes, until turning slightly golden. Add the onions and fry over a lowish heat for 8 minutes, or until they have begun to soften. For the last minute of cooking, add the garlic and thyme.

Remove from the heat and put into a mixing bowl with the sausagemeat, offal, breadcrumbs, parsley, lemon and orange zest, nutmeg, chestnuts, fruit and pistachios and a good sprinkling of salt and pepper. Roll up your sleeves and get squelching it together, really giving it a good mix to make sure it's combined. Put in a bowl and keep it in the fridge until you are ready to use it (see page 173).

Laying the Christmas table

While I'm no stickler for formalities, I do think that Christmas is the one time of the year where it's nice to make a little extra effort. You've put so much time into cooking a delicious meal and entertaining is at the heart of it, so surely you want to do it justice by eating it in a lovely setting? Choose a colour scheme and stick to it – go for something that matches your house decorations. I love colour so I will mix-and-match all colours, Christmassy or not, with a huge handful of gold and bronze thrown in!

You will need:

A TABLECLOTH

A tablecloth is not essential, but it is particularly useful if you are joining tables together to make them look uniform. I love vintage tablecloths. For Christmas I whip out a really stunning dyed lace one my mate Pearl Lowe makes, (www.pearllowe.co.uk).

NAPKINS

I have a pet hate and it's snobby as hell... paper napkins. They make me feel a bit, well... sad. Invest in good-quality napkins that you can wash. They are better for the environment, but importantly look more elegant. You can find really great vintage ones on eBay that have a nod towards Christmas. I like to use some stunning napkins with gold lace stars over them, simply folded or put into a neat napkin ring. Avoid folding them into "interesting" napkin sculptures – simple elegance wins every time.

ADEQUATE CUTLERY

Check you have enough of everything before your guests arrive – there's no shame in asking a family member to bring a little extra. Make sure you have enough knives, forks and spoons for each course, butter knives for side plates, and a selection of serving utensils. I love a mix-and-match vibe and collect a mixture of old and new. I could still do with more, but the closer I get to owning a good collection the more I feel like an actual grown-up!

CROCKERY

Again, check you have enough before your guests arrive. If you are lucky enough to have a lovely set, Christmas is the time to get it out, but I also think a little bit of mix-and-match provides a certain charm. Traditionally you need a small/medium plate for starters, a large (dinner) plate for the main course and a small plate (or bowls) for dessert. I LOVE serving my food "family-style" on massive platters and wooden boards and letting everyone dig in. I think this way is more informal than individual dishes and is a more modern way to serve your food. Serving platters are also really useful in my effort to "bring back the buffet" (you can't have too many as far as I'm concerned). Don't forget about things like gravy jugs (I spent years embarrassingly serving gravy out of a measuring jug!).

I collect things from junk shops, and eBay, and I've been known to steal a few bits from my mum, too. My biggest pet hate is when people layer plates on top of plates. It's so formal, and frankly we're feeding our family, not running a restaurant! There is one recipe in this book where I suggest you cover the table with greaseproof paper and pile the food into the middle to eat (see New England Clambake on page 72). It's liberating – try it!

TABLE MATS

For hot dishes and hot plates on the table only. I'm not personally a fan of the place mat, but each to their own.

PLACE NAMES

This is a great job for the kids to do. I love kids' handwriting – it looks really cute and cool and, well… it brings a family touch. If there isn't anyone to write your guests' names for you, then just write them in your best handwriting and attach each tag to a sprig of rosemary and glue on a few fresh cranberries.

CHRISTMAS CRACKERS

In the UK these are a must! At least one for every person. Don't spend too much money on them, the quality-versus-value ratio is just not worth it, but find a happy medium if you can. And make sure they match your colour scheme.

CANDLES

Candlelight automatically creates a special atmosphere and the flattering ambient light makes everyone look nice! DO use a mixture of church candles, tealights and long candles. DO NOT use scented candles as they will overwhelm your palate and mar the flavours of the food.

FLOWERS & TABLE DECORATIONS

Some festive flowers or greenery on the table is a lovely touch. I love to scatter the table with natural things such as pine cones, chestnuts, fresh cranberries, sprigs of holly and mistletoe, but I also add a bit of pizzazz with some table glitter or tiny stars. Again avoid anything scented – you'll be amazed at how the smell of flowers can affect your taste buds.

LAYING THE TABLE

If using a tablecloth, align the centre crease along the centre of the table. If using table mats, position them an equal distance apart and make sure everyone has enough room – there's nothing worse that having elbows in your Christmas dinner. Arrange the chairs around the table with this in mind, too. Place folded napkins on plates. Tie up each knife and fork using pretty ribbon and decorations such as holly or baubles and place on

top of each napkin. Alternatively, position the knives and forks for each course alongside each place setting, with the cutlery for the first course on the outside and the cutlery for dessert on the inside. Knives should be on the right side facing inwards, forks on the left. Dessert spoons should sit to the left of the knives. Place any glasses above the cutlery. Arrange the place names and a Christmas cracker above each setting. Now you can arrange any candles, flowers, or extra decorations along the middle of the table, leaving space for serving dishes. Don't overcrowd the table though, you don't want to be worrying about knocking things over when you're trying to tuck in! It's nice to have condiments placed at each end of the table with a couple of little spoons so that there isn't too much passing around. Same goes for gravy jugs.

CHESTNUT, APPLE & PRUNE STUFFING
(FOR GOOSE OR DUCK)

300ml (10fl oz) hot orange juice

100ml (3½fl oz) hot water

50ml (2fl oz) Armagnac

150g (3½oz) prunes

1 tablespoon unsalted butter

6 smoked streaky bacon rashers, chopped

1 onion, finely chopped

3 garlic cloves, finely chopped

a few thyme sprigs, leaves picked

300g (10½oz) sausagemeat (or good-quality sausages, squeezed out of their skins)

the goose offal (liver and kidneys), roughly chopped (optional)

a handful of fresh white breadcrumbs

2 tablespoons finely chopped parsley

200g (7oz) peeled vacuum-packed chestnuts, roughly chopped

1 large English apple, grated

sea salt flakes and freshly ground black pepper

Pour the hot orange juice into a bowl and add the hot water, Armagnac and prunes. Leave to soak overnight. Next day, strain the prunes (discarding any excess liquid), then roughly chop and set aside.

Heat the butter in a frying pan. Add the bacon and fry for 5 minutes, until turning slightly golden. Add the onion and fry over a low-ish heat for 8 minutes, or until it has begun to soften. For the last minute of cooking, add the garlic and thyme.

Remove from the heat and put into a large mixing bowl with the sausagemeat, offal, breadcrumbs, parsley, chestnuts, apple, prunes and a good sprinkling of salt and pepper. Roll up your sleeves and get squelching it together, really giving it a good mix to make sure it's combined. Put it in a bowl and keep it in the fridge until you are ready to use it.

Stuffing whole birds

There is a lot of controversy about stuffing birds. Do you put the stuffing in the cavity, or must it go under the skin? Is stuffing a bird risky, and should you avoid it completely and bake the stuffing separately in balls or a tin? Well, the answer has to be: do whatever you feel comfortable with; just make sure the stuffing is piping hot when you serve it, or it may not be cooked properly.

I have always stuffed my birds in the cavity, as my mother did, and as did hers, and none of us have ever had any trouble. I choose this technique because, when the turkey cooks and rests, the juices ooze into the stuffing, which really benefits from this extra moisture and flavour.

The usual advice given is that if you want to be cautious, stuff under the skin; those who are really nervous shouldn't stuff the bird at all and should cook the stuffing separately. All ways are fine, but there is one rule: whichever way you choose to do it, you must account for the stuffing in the weight of the bird when working out your cooking times, so weigh the bird after it has been stuffed.

It is also unusual to stuff any bird other than a chicken or turkey under the skin, as the skin tends to be either too thick or too thin, so if you want to stuff a goose or duck, for example, go for the cavity or cook the stuffing separately.

Stuffing the carcass

Tip the bird so the cavity is facing upwards and wide open. Take fistfuls of the stuffing and push it into the cavity. Fill the bird up, then round the stuffing off at the end, making sure you don't overstuff it because the bird will push a little stuffing out as it cooks.

Stuffing under the skin

From the neck end of the bird, carefully slide your hands under the skin to detach it from the meat – this is surprisingly easy and you can even detach the skin from the leg meat if you're careful. (This is a great technique if you're going to rub the bird with butter to add moisture while cooking.) If you want to add stuffing under the skin, spread it evenly, smoothing it out as you go to create a really thin layer (around 5–8mm/¼–⅜ inch). It will make the bird appear quite odd whole, but it looks really impressive when you carve the breast meat into slices.

Cooking stuffing separately

Either shape your stuffing into balls, or press it into a buttered loaf tin, so that you can carve it into slices (like a terrine) when cooked. You can also line the loaf tin with streaky bacon or wrap each ball in smoked streaky bacon to keep it moist while cooking. Bake with the turkey for 30–40 minutes.

SERVES 8–10, WITH LEFTOVERS

PREPARATION TIME: 30 MINUTES, PLUS RESTING

COOKING TIME: 2½ HOURS

NEIL'S ROAST RIB OF BEEF
WITH MUSTARD GRAVY

I want to give you guys the best cooking instructions I know, so I find myself again quizzing the brilliant Neil Rankin. If you've read my recipe for Spiced Dry-brined Turkey (see page 160) you will already know that Neil has shared his advice on cooking the perfect turkey at a terrifyingly low cooking temperature. It works perfectly, and the same method is introduced here (though in this case browning the meat beforehand is essential). The idea is that when cooking something more slowly it cooks more evenly, and therefore the meat is juicier and much more tender. Like Neil, I'm a believer that good meat doesn't need too much other flavour added, and have simply opted for a really good salty crust, but served it with a flavour-infused proper mustard gravy. You HAVE to use fresh stock for this gravy. A stock cube won't do, and while it's super-easy to make, you can buy really good freshly made stocks from the chiller cabinet at the supermarket these days. I've also tagged on a recipe for the easiest Fresh Horseradish Cream. If you've not used horseradish fresh before, it will blow your mind (maybe quite literally, as it's pretty pokey).

1 x 5kg (11lb) tied rib of beef with rib cap and a thick layer of fat

sea salt flakes

For the mustard gravy

vegetable oil

5 shallots, sliced

1 carrot, chopped

1 stick of celery, chopped

1 teaspoon plain flour

400ml (14fl oz) red wine

450ml (16fl oz) Madeira or port

75ml (2¾fl oz) brandy

2 litres (3½ pints) fresh beef or brown chicken stock, plus any pan juices from the roast

3 bay leaves (rip the leaves a little to release more flavour)

2 thyme sprigs

4 black peppercorns

6 garlic cloves, crushed

2 tablespoons English mustard

50g (1¾oz) unsalted butter

sea salt flakes

Get yourself a roasting pan big enough to hold the rib of beef and heat your oven to 140°C/120°C fan (275°F) Gas Mark 1.

Put the pan on the hob over a medium heat, and slowly render the fat on the rib roast. Once the pan fills up with fat, pour it into a suitable container and reserve it. Keep cooking the meat until you have about 400ml (14fl oz) of reserved fat. If you can't get enough fat off the rib, top it up with vegetable oil. Once this is done, increase the heat and give the beef some nice deep colour on all sides, seasoning with crushed sea salt flakes as you go. Take your time with this, as it will make all the difference to the final depth of the meat's flavour.

Once browned, place in the oven and cook for 2½ hours for medium-rare. Remove from the oven and leave to rest uncovered for 30 minutes. Collect all the juices and reserve for the gravy, and use the beef fat for your Beef-dripping Yorkshires (see page 176) or Perfect Roast Potatoes (see page 179).

To make the gravy, heat the vegetable oil over a medium heat. Throw all the vegetables into the pan, and cook down until they are nicely caramelized. Add the flour and cook for another minute, then add the red wine, Madeira or port and brandy and simmer until reduced to half its volume. Pour in the stock and keep simmering until reduced by half again (skim as the stock is coming to the boil, and then as often as you can).

Next add the bay leaves, thyme, peppercorns and garlic, and keep simmering until you have the desired consistency. I don't like my gravy too thick, but on the other hand there's nothing worse than watery gravy! The best way to assess this is to taste the gravy. You want it to taste rich and full of flavour. Finally, add the mustard, butter and salt to taste, whisking to make sure the butter is emulsified into the sauce.

To carve the beef, remove the chine bone and ribs and slice, seasoning each slice with a little salt. Serve with the gravy and horseradish and the same Christmas veggies you would have with the turkey.

SERVES 8–10
PREPARATION TIME: 20 MINUTES
COOKING TIME: NONE

FRESH HORSERADISH CREAM

15g (½oz) finely grated fresh horseradish
1 tablespoon white wine vinegar
a pinch of English mustard powder
½ teaspoon golden caster sugar
sea salt flakes and freshly ground black pepper
150ml (5fl oz) double cream, lightly whipped

Soak the horseradish in 2 tablespoons of boiling water and leave until cool. Drain, then mix with the rest of the ingredients. Leave in the fridge to soften for at least 20 minutes before using.

BEEF-DRIPPING YORKSHIRES

There is a simple rule for Yorkshires. It's equal quantities of flour, eggs and milk. I like them simple and unflavoured except for a little salt and really good beef dripping, just like Neil…

200ml (7fl oz) plain flour

200ml (7fl oz) free-range eggs (about 4 medium eggs, but see method)

200ml (7fl oz) milk

400ml (14fl oz) rendered fat from the rib of beef, but you can buy beef dripping from good butchers

sea salt flakes

The easiest way to do this (with the least washing up!) is to use a measuring jug instead of scales to measure out all your ingredients. Start with the flour and transfer it to a bowl, then measure the same volume of eggs, then the same volume of milk. Beat together until smooth, but don't be too worried if there are a few lumps. Leave the batter at room temperature for an hour or so, or in the fridge overnight.

When you are ready to cook your puddings, preheat the oven to 220°C/200°C fan (425°F), Gas Mark 7. Add a good pinch of salt to the batter. Pour a decent amount (around 1 tablespoon) of your reserved beef dripping into each cup of a muffin tray.

The trick here is to get the fat really hot, so put the tray into the oven and heat for a good 5 minutes. At this point, open the oven door and carefully pour the batter into the muffin tray. I'd suggest about 2 tablespoons each, but the more batter the bigger the pudding!

Bake for about 20 minutes, or until risen and golden. If you're not cooking a million things at once, it's a good idea to turn off your oven and leave the puddings inside for another 5 minutes to dry out a little.

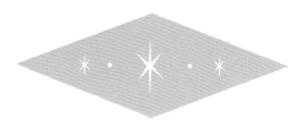

My ultimate Christmas playlist

These tunes are my favourite mix of old classics and cover versions to get me in the festive mood.

"All I Want for Christmas Is You" Mariah Carey

"Away In A Manger" Bing Crosby

"Christmas Story" Doris Day

"Christmas Time is Here" Vince Guaraldi Trio

"Frosty the Snowman" Beach Boys

"I Saw Mommy Kissing Santa Claus" Ronnettes

"I've Got My Love to Keep Me Warm" Billie Holliday

"Last Christmas" Wham

"Let it Snow!" Dean Martin

"O, Come All Ye Faithful" Nat King Cole

"Rockin' Around the Christmas Tree" Brenda Lee

"Santa Baby" Eartha Kitt

"Santa Claus is Coming to Town" The Crystals

"Silent Night" Frank Sinatra

"Sleigh Ride" The Ronnettes

"Sometime At Christmas" Stevie Wonder

"Soulful Christmas" James Brown

"The Twelve Days of Christmas" Connie Francis

"White Christmas" Peggy Lee

"Winter Wonderland" The Judds

PERFECT ROAST POTATOES

I always vowed I'd never mess about with roast potatoes. Now I still feel like this, but I have to hand it to the addition of a few flavours: garlic and rosemary can make all the difference. I feel strongly about the fat as well: I don't think you should use entirely goose or duck fat or dripping. I think it needs to be lightened with some vegetable oil. Otherwise it's just too rich and the potatoes don't crisp up as much. This way you get the best of both worlds: a hint of flavour and super-crispness. The other tip is that the best roasties have been parboiled and shaken to fluff up the edges for crispness, but then left to steam until almost cool before being thrown into scorching hot fat. Follow the recipe for outstandingly good roast spuds!

6 largish potatoes, peeled and quartered

6 tablespoons 50:50 vegetable oil and goose fat, for the perfect mix of crispness and flavour

a few rosemary sprigs

1 garlic bulb, halved horizontally

sea salt flakes

Preheat the oven to 220°C/200°C fan (425°F), Gas Mark 7. Place the potatoes in a large pan and cover them with cold water. Add 1 teaspoon of salt. Bring to the boil, then parboil for 7 minutes, until the potatoes are a bit "furry" or flaky on the outside but still firm and uncooked in the middle. Drain them and give them a bit of a shake in the colander or sieve so the edges become grainy – this will give you the crispiest potatoes. Leave them to "steam" for 15 minutes, to remove the excess water and make them extra fluffy all the way through.

Pour the fats into a large baking tray, and pop it into the oven to heat for 5 minutes. Tip the drained, "steamed", parboiled potatoes into the hot fat. Turn them to make sure each potato is coated in the oil. Add the rosemary and garlic and roast in the oven for 50 minutes, turning them every 15–20 minutes.

Remove the potatoes with a slotted spoon and drain on kitchen paper. Sprinkle generously with sea salt flakes before serving.

VEGETARIAN HAGGIS WELLINGTON

No one can convince me that a nut roast is delicious. I love vegetarian food, I really do, but nut roast feels so dated and dense I can't get my head around it. I've tried and failed at many "brilliant" nut roast recipes, so I really have given it some welly. The one thing I fell for a while back was vegetarian haggis. Oddly the recipe was in a similar vein to the nut roast, but it's lighter and has more texture and its spicing is just far superior. I thought, how can we make the humble haggis "fancy" and "Christmassy"? Make it into a Wellington – that's how! So here it is – to be served with mashed swede, and ALL the Christmas trimmings. It's brilliant with Gingerbread Sauce (see page 195), Cranberry, Port & Clementine Sauce (see page 194) and this really great vegetarian gravy... See photograph on page 181.

2 tablespoons olive oil

6 shallots, finely chopped

5 Portabello mushrooms, very finely chopped

5 chestnut mushrooms, very finely chopped

3 garlic cloves, finely chopped

1 tablespoons fresh rosemary leaves, finely chopped

1 tablespoon truffle oil (optional)

2 x 340g (11¾oz) vegetarian haggis (I use Macsween)

plain flour, for dusting

1 x 320g (11½ oz) packet of ready rolled, all-butter puff pastry

2 large free-range egg yolks, beaten

Heat the oil in a large frying pan over a medium heat. Add the shallots and let them begin to soften. After 2–3 minutes, add the mushrooms and fry for a further 10–15 minutes, until they have softened and browned. Add the garlic, rosemary and truffle oil (if using), and fry for a further minute. Be sure to cook off any juices, as it is important this mixture is not too wet. Remove from the heat and leave to cool.

Remove the haggis from their packaging, and trim the ends so they are the same diameter all the way along. Lay out a double layer of clingfilm about 40cm (16 inches) long, and then a second one, placing it about 10cm (4 inches) lower than the top edge of the first one to create a wide rectangle that will cover the circumference of the Wellington. Spread the mushroom mixture out in a neat rectangle long enough and wide enough to go around the haggis (about 40 x 30cm/16 x 12 inches) and pat down evenly with your hands. Place the 2 haggis end-to end at the top of this rectangle and then, using the clingfilm, carefully and tightly roll into a cylinder, twisting the ends like a cracker. Pop into the fridge to chill for 30 minutes.

Roll the pastry out on a floured surface into a 40 x 30cm (16 x 12 inch) rectangle. Unravel the mushroom-covered haggis from the clingfilm and lay it across a long side of the pastry, then roll it up. Trim off any excess from each end and fold neatly underneath the haggis. You can roll out any extra pastry and cut into shapes, such as jazzy stars! Brush the pastry all over with the beaten egg. Decorate with the pastry shapes and glaze these with the remaining egg, too. Now chill the Wellington in the fridge for 30 minutes.

For the vegetarian gravy

2 tablespoons rapeseed oil

1 onion, thinly sliced

1 carrot, thinly sliced

1 teaspoon tomato purée

1 teaspoon dark brown sugar

2 tablespoons plain flour

1 small glass of red wine

1 litre (1¾ pints) vegetable stock
   (fresh is best, but if not available,
   use low-salt veg bouillon powder)

2 bay leaves

1 teaspoon–1 tablespoon Marmite

sea salt flakes and freshly ground
   black pepper

Heat the oven to 200°C/180°C fan (400°F), Gas Mark 6. Bake the Wellington for 35–40 minutes, or until the pastry is crisp and golden.

Meanwhile, you can get on with the gravy. Heat the oil in a medium pan and throw in the onion and carrot. Fry over a medium heat for about 10 minutes, or until softened and getting a little caramelized. Add the tomato purée and brown sugar and ramp up the heat. Fry for a minute, until the vegetables are caramelized, then add the flour. Stir-fry the flour for another minute, then pour in the wine. Let it bubble away for a minute until it's almost evaporated, then pour over the stock slowly, stirring constantly until it's all combined. Add the bay leaves and Marmite to taste and let it simmer slowly for about 15 minutes, or until thickened. Season with plenty of salt and pepper. Strain the gravy back into a clean pan and bring back to the boil – it should have a pouring consistency, like single cream, or… erm… gravy. Serve the Wellington in slices with the piping hot gravy.

- SERVES 4
- PREPARATION TIME: 15 MINUTES
- COOKING TIME: 45 MINUTES

BRAISED SOUR RED CABBAGE

WITH POMEGRANATE

My mum's red cabbage beats everyone else's. GAHHH! We all think things like this, don't we! I don't know whether when I make these statements people accept them or find them irritating or become over-protective of their own mum's dishes. I mean, I eat a lot of food, and a lot of food that people claim is the best version, but I still think when I say that my mum makes the best version of something, I really and truly mean it. Red cabbage is one of my mum's great side dishes. We have it with everything from sausages to pork chops to Christmas lunch. She's half Polish, so a lightly pickled hot red cabbage is second nature to her. I have already published her recipe in my book, ***Gizzi's Kitchen Magic***. Here I've taken the essence of her recipe, but made it more Christmassy with the inclusion of seasonal pomegranates, both in the braise and at the end to finish it. It's a vibrant, acidic necessity with your Christmas lunch.

- 2 tablespoons olive oil
- 2 red onions, thinly sliced
- ½ large red cabbage (or 1 small one), cored and thinly sliced
- 100ml (3½fl oz) red wine vinegar
- 150ml (5fl oz) water
- 3 tablespoons brown sugar
- 50ml (2fl oz) pomegranate molasses
- 3 juniper berries
- a pinch of ground cloves
- seeds from ½ pomegranate
- sea salt flakes and freshly ground black pepper

Heat the olive oil in a large pan (I use a wok) and fry the onions gently for 8 minutes, or until they have softened and started to get a golden tinge. Add the cabbage and stir-fry for a further 5 minutes.

Pour over the vinegar, water and sugar, and stir until the sugar has dissolved. Add the molasses and spices, then pop a lid on and let it slowly simmer for 40 minutes. You may need to check the water level at this stage. What you're looking for is that, when you move the cabbage away with a spoon, it slowly leaves a drool of lightly syrupy liquid. You don't want it too dry, but not too wet either. Season with salt and pepper and stir through the pomegranate seeds before serving.

SERVES 8

PREPARATION TIME: 15 MINUTES

COOKING TIME: 40 MINUTES

REALLY SIMPLE HONEY GLAZED CARROTS & PARSNIPS

I really don't like to mess about with veggies too much. Already on your Christmas plate you have sprouts with all kinds of jazz, and possibly a really flavoursome red cabbage, so I believe you should keep the rest simple. This carrot and parsnip combo is simply roasted with honey and no fuss, but will still be perfectly cooked and the honey will bring out the natural flavours.

2 tablespoons unsalted butter
or olive oil

500g (1lb 2oz) small to medium
carrots, peeled but kept whole with
a little bit of green "hair" left on

500g (1lb 2oz) parsnips, peeled,
cut into quarters lengthways,
and parboiled for 5 minutes

4 tablespoons honey

a few thyme sprigs (but only
if you like...)

sea salt flakes and freshly ground
black pepper

Preheat the oven to 220°C/200°C fan (425°F), Gas Mark 7.

Pour the butter or oil into a roasting tray and place in the oven to heat up for 5–10 minutes. When hot, remove from the oven and add the carrots and parsnips. Drizzle over the honey and a decent splash of water. Season with salt and pepper and add the thyme sprigs (if using).

Give the carrots and parsnips a good toss to make sure they are evenly coated in the oil and honey, then place in the oven and roast for 30 minutes, giving them a good stir halfway through. You want the vegetables to be cooked through and lightly caramelized, but still retain some bite.

SPROUTS THREE WAYS

Sprouts are the cast-offs of the Christmas lunch plate. For me, they get a bad rep. I adore them. The true flavour of a sprout is maybe a little more iron-y than most can bear, and it's true that they have a distinctive spicy, maybe even mustardy tang to them, but when this is embraced and the sprout is allowed to reach its full potential, they are fantastic. So here are three ways to get the best out of them. What I like to do on Christmas Day is make the creamed sprouts with nutmeg, then top a dish of this with the stir-fried Sprouts, Smoked Bacon & Chestnuts. With each scoop you get creamy comforting sprouts and then slightly charred ones with sweet chestnuts and smoky bacon. The rest of the time I enjoy sprouts cooked in any of these ways, as well as the Shredded Sprout Salads (see page 62).

SERVES 6-8

PREPARATION TIME: 10 MINUTES

COOKING TIME: 10 MINUTES

SPROUTS, SMOKED BACON & CHESTNUTS

It's classic, but classic for a reason.

500g (1lb 2oz) small Brussels sprouts

a knob of unsalted butter

150g (5½oz) pancetta, cut into strips

250g (9oz) vacuum-packed chestnuts

sea salt flakes and freshly ground black pepper

Trim the sprouts, halve or quarter them, then cook them in boiling water for 2–3 minutes, until just done. For me this is when they are most definitely cooked through but still have a decent amount of crunch. Drain. Heat the butter in a wok and fry the pancetta until crisp and golden. Add the chestnuts and sprouts and stir-fry for 3–4 minutes. Finally add salt and pepper and serve.

ROAST SPROUTS
WITH BALSAMIC GLAZE &
ROASTED HAZELNUTS

✳ SERVES 6–8
✳ PREPARATION TIME: 10 MINUTES
✳ COOKING TIME: 25–30 MINUTES

Roasting sprouts sweetens them, and the charred caramelization they are left with makes them all the sweeter.

500g (1lb 2oz) small Brussels sprouts

2 tablespoons olive oil

3 tablespoons balsamic vinegar

100g (3½oz) skinned hazelnuts

2 tablespoons roasted hazelnut oil (optional)

sea salt flakes and freshly ground black pepper

Heat the oven to 200°C/180°C fan (400°F), Gas Mark 6. Trim the sprouts, place them in a roasting tray, and toss with the olive oil, balsamic and 50ml (2fl oz) of water. Roast the sprouts in the oven for 20 minutes, then stir, add the hazelnuts and roast for a further 5–10 minutes or until the hazelnuts are golden brown. Season with salt and pepper. Dress with the roasted hazelnut oil before serving, if using.

CREAMED SPROUTS
WITH NUTMEG

✳ SERVES 6–8
✳ PREPARATION TIME: 10 MINUTES
✳ COOKING TIME: 10 MINUTES

Sprout purée may seem quite radical, but this comes from the same place as creamed spinach. I add some Parmesan for extra flavour – it's a really ambrosial way of eating sprouts.

500g (1lb 2oz) Brussels sprouts

150ml (5fl oz) crème fraîche

20g (¾oz) Parmesan cheese, finely grated

20g (¾oz) butter

a really good pinch of freshly grated nutmeg

sea salt flakes and freshly ground black pepper

Trim the sprouts, halve or quarter them, then cook them in boiling water for 4–5 minutes, until cooked through and softening a little more than if you were eating them whole. Drain, then leave to steam for another 5 minutes. This makes them drier and steams them so they are cooked evenly. Place them in a food processor with the crème fraîche, Parmesan, butter, nutmeg and seasoning and blitz until smooth(ish). Put back into the saucepan over a medium heat and reheat until piping hot. Check the seasoning and serve.

CRANBERRY, PORT & CLEMENTINE SAUCE

Cranberry sauce should be a sauce, not with a jammy or jelly consistency like the shop-bought ones. It should be cranberries floating in a fruity syrup – a fairly clingy, not watery syrup, but a syrup all the same. I like mine warm, just a spot cooler than bread sauce. It's how it's meant to be served.

500g (1lb 2oz) fresh cranberries
80g (2¾oz) golden caster sugar
100ml (3½fl oz) ruby red port
juice of 2 clementines and finely grated zest of ½ clementine

Place the cranberries, sugar, port, clementine juice and zest in a small saucepan over a high heat, stirring while it comes to the boil. Once it's boiling, reduce the heat and let it simmer away for 5–10 minutes, or until the cranberries have all started to pop and release their juice. You want the cranberries swimming in sauce – it's ready when the sauce is a pouring but very syrupy texture. Don't stir it too much. You want to keep some of the berries whole, only allowing a few to break up. Give the pan the odd swizzle and scrape at the bottom, but avoid a proper stir.

When it's ready, leave to cool in the pan and serve warm with turkey, duck, venison, baked Brie... whatever you fancy.

GINGERBREAD SAUCE

Christmas is not Christmas without bread sauce. I've thrown a fit before when my mum forgot to make it and the whole Christmas lunch was held up while it was made due to my extreme tantrum, and I'm not at all embarrassed. When people say they don't like it, I'm perplexed for a second, but then happy because there is more for me. Bread sauce when done properly is not the claggy, lumpy stuff many people think of – it's loose and can be poured, it's full of spicy flavour and sits between turkey, stuffing, gravy and cranberry sauce like a five-piece pop band. They are all great on their own, but together they give so much more! In this recipe I've included warming ginger for a real Hansel and Gretel gingerbread feel. It's now even more delicious.

600ml (20fl oz) milk

50g (1¾oz) unsalted butter

1 onion, chopped

6 cloves

6 peppercorns

1 bay leaf

100g (3½oz) fresh white breadcrumbs

4 tablespoons double cream or mascarpone

¼ teaspoon ground ginger

¼ teaspoon freshly grated nutmeg

¼ teaspoon ground allspice

¼ teaspoon ground cloves

sea salt flakes and freshly ground black pepper

Put the milk, butter, onion, cloves, peppercorns and bay leaf into a pan and bring to the boil, then reduce the heat to a simmer. Cook gently for 5 minutes, then leave to infuse for 1 hour.

Strain the liquid and return it to the pan. Add the breadcrumbs and simmer for 3–4 minutes. Stir in the cream or mascarpone. Add the spices and season. The sauce is ready when it has a thick pouring consistency and is full of spicy flavour. If you make this in advance it will thicken up a bit, but it can be loosened with more milk and reheated ready to be served.

A WREATH OF PIGS IN BLANKETS

I don't want to mess around with pigs in blankets too much, so this is merely a beautiful serving suggestion. My best advice is to buy the best smoked bacon you can afford and real butcher's sausages. After that, it's about getting creative. You can make this a day in advance and keep it tightly covered in the fridge until ready to roast. I use it as a centrepiece on the table and stick a bowl in the middle filled with anything from cranberry sauce to roast potatoes.

18 smoked streaky bacon rashers

18 traditional butcher's sausages
  (I like Cumberland or Lincolnshire)

18 toothpicks

12 bay leaves

8 rosemary sprigs

a good few thyme sprigs

oil (I would use rapeseed), for cooking

Cranberry, Port & Clementine Sauce
  (see page 194), to serve

Preheat the oven to 220°C/200°C fan (425°F), Gas Mark 7. Get the largest chopping board you have. The first thing to do is to wrap the sausages in the bacon. I think they look best with a bit of sausage peeping out at each end. Lay a slice of bacon flat on the chopping board and roll a sausage up in it. Don't wrap it too tight, but make sure it's firmly wrapped. Repeat with the rest of the sausages.

Now it's time to make your "wreath". Line a baking sheet with greaseproof paper. Place a side plate bang in the centre of the paper and draw round the edge in pencil. This is just to ensure you try and stick to some kind of circle shape and don't go 'off piste' and make an oval wreath. Lay the wrapped sausages around in a tight circle.

Next up, it's time to secure the wreath so it doesn't fall apart. Push a toothpick in each bit of sausage where it is sitting closest to the next sausage to secure it to its next 3 neighbours; repeat by doing the same thing to the next sausage along, following the circle round until your wreath of sausages is all held together.

OK, so you now have your base wreath. Get all your herbs and intertwine them through the wreath. Drizzle with oil and bake in the oven for 30–35 minutes, or until the sausages and bacon are golden and cooked through. Remove from the oven and transfer to a serving board or platter, then remove the toothpicks. You can serve the wreath on its own, or put a bowl filled with Cranberry, Port & Clemintine Sauce in the middle for dipping and use it as a centrepiece on your dining table.

※ SERVES 8

※ PREPARATION TIME 45 MINUTES,
   PLUS COOLING AND CHILLING

※ COOKING TIME 1 HOUR

CLEMENTINE & GINGER TRIFLE

Christmas wouldn't be Christmas without trifle for most people, but I have to confess, our family didn't eat trifle, not just at Christmas, but ever... It seems like madness, as we're all MONSTER trifle-eaters now, but it was a slow start for my sisters and me. The good thing is I'm not a trifle purist, and I actually think many recipes could be improved (hides)! So here we have my take on the Christmas trifle, with an old-school clementine jelly and a classic ginger cake, made boozy with ginger liqueur. Thick custard, cream, glacé cherries and chocolate. It's epic. I hope you enjoy!

100ml (3½fl oz) ginger liqueur
  (I use The King's Ginger liqueur)
600ml (20fl oz) fresh custard
300ml (10fl oz) double cream
1 teaspoon icing sugar
50g (1¾oz) good-quality dark chocolate
a few glacé cherries, chopped

For the ginger cake

225g (8oz) unsalted butter, plus extra
  for buttering the tin
225g (8oz) dark brown sugar
225g (8oz) black treacle
2 free-range eggs, beaten
290ml (9¾fl oz) milk
340g (11¾oz) plain flour
1 tablespoon ground ginger
1 tablespoon ground cinnamon
a small fresh grating of nutmeg
2 teaspoons bicarbonate of soda

For the clementine jelly

150ml (5fl oz) water
50g (1¾oz) caster sugar
300ml (10fl oz) clementine juice
4 gelatine leaves
3 clementines, segmented

First make the ginger cake: preheat the oven to 180°C/160°C fan (350°F), Gas Mark 4. Butter and line a 30 x 20cm (12 x 8 inch) roasting tin. Melt the butter, sugar and treacle together in a pan, leave to cool for 10 minutes, then stir in the eggs and milk. Sift the flour, ginger, cinnamon, nutmeg and bicarbonate of soda together in a large mixing bowl, then fold in the butter mixture to form a batter. Pour into the prepared tin and bake for 45 minutes, or until the cake is risen and firm. Leave to cool on a wire rack and store in an airtight container until needed. You will have made too much cake, but this is NO disaster – it freezes brilliantly and gets better with age.

To make the clementine jelly, put the water, sugar and clementine juice into a small saucepan. Soak the gelatine leaves in cold water for 10 minutes, then squeeze out any water with your hands and add to the clementine juice to dissolve. Arrange the clementine segments in the bottom of your trifle bowl, pour over the liquid and refrigerate for at least 4 hours, to set.

Now you're ready to construct the trifle. Chop up 150g (5½oz) of the cake and place on top of the jelly. Pour over the ginger liqueur. Pour over the custard and level out the top. Whisk the cream with the icing sugar until it's gently holding its shape, then spoon over the custard. Grate over the chocolate and finish with glacé cherries if you like. Pop the trifle into the fridge to chill for 1 hour before eating.

* SERVES 6
* PREPARATION TIME: 30 MINUTES
* COOKING TIME: 2½ HOURS,
  PLUS COOLING

GRAPEFRUIT CURD
PAVLOVA

The base of this pavlova is a recipe by my beloved Meringue Girls. They do a really clever trick in roasting the sugar and adding it to the whipping egg whites, which makes a much more stable, marshmallowy meringue that cooks to that perfect crunchy outside and chewy middle. I've topped the pavlova with THE MOST BRILLIANT grapefruit curd, and some caramelized dehydrated grapefruit thins. It's fine, grown-up and elegant, but with cheeky hints of sherbet and bitter-sweetness – it looks so damn Christmassy and makes a superb centrepiece pudding for this kind of special occasion.

For the meringue

300g (10½oz) caster sugar

5 free-range eggs

For the caramelized grapefruit

3 grapefruit, 1 pink, 1 red and 1 white, peeled and thinly sliced using a mandolin

1 tablespoon caster sugar

For the grapefruit curd

150ml (5fl oz) strained grapefruit juice

50ml (2fl oz) lemon juice

75g (2¾oz) golden caster sugar

1 free-range egg (I use Cotswold Legbars or Burford Browns, for their orange yolks)

75g (2¾oz) unsalted butter, chopped

For the whipped cream topping

300ml (10fl oz) double cream

1 teaspoon seeded vanilla extract

1 teaspoon icing sugar

To make the meringue, preheat the oven to 220°C/200°C fan (425°F), Gas Mark 7. Line a large flat baking sheet with baking parchment.

Line a deep roasting tray with baking parchment, then pour in the sugar and put it into the oven for about 5 minutes, until the edges are about to melt. Heating the sugar helps to create a more stable, glossy mixture. Separate the eggs (set 4 of the yolks aside for the curd) and put the whites into a large, clean bowl. Using a free-standing mixer or electric hand whisk, begin to whisk them slowly, allowing small bubbles to form, then increase the speed gradually until they form stiff peaks.

Reduce the oven temperature to 120°C/100°C fan (250°F), Gas Mark ½. Still whisking at speed, add the hot sugar to the egg whites 1 spoonful at a time. Once you have added all the sugar, continue to whisk for a further 5–7 minutes, until the sugar has dissolved and the mixture is smooth, stiff and glossy.

Spread the mixture on the prepared baking sheet in a fat circle approximately 23cm (9 inches) in diameter. Make a well in the centre. Cook in the oven for 2 hours, then turn the oven off and leave to cool in the oven for 1 hour, with the door a little ajar.

At the same time, to make the caramelized grapefruit thins, place the sliced grapefruit on a baking sheet lined with baking parchment and sprinkle with the caster sugar. Place in the bottom of the oven while the meringue is cooking. They will be caramelized and dehydrated after 1–2 hours. Keep an eye on them to make sure the sugar doesn't scorch. Remove from the baking sheet straight away and place on a wire rack where they will continue to dehydrate and crisp up.

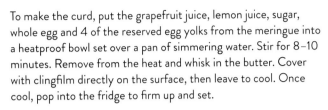

To make the curd, put the grapefruit juice, lemon juice, sugar, whole egg and 4 of the reserved egg yolks from the meringue into a heatproof bowl set over a pan of simmering water. Stir for 8–10 minutes. Remove from the heat and whisk in the butter. Cover with clingfilm directly on the surface, then leave to cool. Once cool, pop into the fridge to firm up and set.

Whip the cream with the vanilla and icing sugar until thick enough to hold its shape, but still soft – there is nothing worse than foamy over-whipped cream.

Remove the meringue from the oven when it's ready and leave to cool to room temperature, but you don't want to leave it anywhere too cold.

Remove the meringue from the baking parchment and transfer to a nice serving plate. Smooth over the whipped cream with a palette knife, followed by the grapefruit curd. Finally, arrange the dried grapefruit thins prettily on top and serve.

MAKES 3 X 1 LITRE (1¾ PINT) PUDDINGS

 PREPARATION TIME: 30 MINUTES,
PLUS SOAKING AND MATURING

 COOKING TIME: 3 HOURS IN ADVANCE,
PLUS 1½ HOURS ON THE DAY

THE BEST CHRISTMAS PUDDING IN THE WORLD!

Christmas pudding is a serious business in the Erskine household. This recipe is inspired by my mother, but the truth is she has totally swiped it from her favourite writers! The basis of it comes from her very favourite food writer (and mine) the pretty much untouchable Robert Carrier, but the rest is a combination of inspiration from the formidable Fanny Cradock and my own hands. Since this is a time to celebrate tradition, this recipe is quite rightly rooted in all my memories of Christmases past. The method requires investing a little time, but it's so worth it to achieve the authentic depth of flavour you would expect from a proper pudding. Neither I nor my mum like nuts in our Christmas pudding, but feel free to add some almonds or walnuts if you prefer. These puddings will keep for over a year if you leave them untouched, and only get better with time.

350g (12oz) sultanas

350g (12oz) raisins

350g (12oz) currants

115g (4oz) chopped mixed peel
  (use the best quality you can buy)

35g (1¼oz) chopped stem ginger, plus
  1 tablespoon of gingery syrup from the jar

2 teaspoons ground allspice

2 teaspoons mixed spice

½ teaspoon freshly grated nutmeg

½ teaspoons salt

6–8 tablespoons brandy

150ml (¼ pint) stout

55g (2oz) grated carrot

1 grated apple

finely grated zest and juice of 1 orange

finely grated zest and juice of 1 lemon

2 tablespoons golden syrup
  or black treacle

225g (8oz) soft dark brown sugar

115g (4oz) self-raising flour

350g (12oz) shredded suet

225g (8oz) fresh white breadcrumbs

4 large free-range eggs, beaten

unsalted butter, to butter the basins

In a large bowl, assemble the dried fruits, peel, ginger and syrup, spices, salt, brandy, stout, carrot, apple, orange and lemon zest and juice and golden syrup (or treacle) and give it a mix with some serious welly. Cover with a tea towel and leave to absorb the booze overnight. Some people like to leave it for a week! I find 2 days is perfect for me, though. Sometimes when you leave it too long it starts to dry out again...

When you're ready to make the puddings, add the dry ingredients to the boozy fruit mixture and stir them all together until fully combined, then stir in the beaten eggs. (Don't forget to make a wish with the last 3 stirs!)

Butter 3 x 1 litre (1¾ pint) pudding basins and line the bottoms with rounds of greaseproof paper. Divide the mixture evenly between the prepared basins, leaving about 2cm (¾ inch) to spare and levelling off the top. Cover the top of each with a round of greaseproof paper to sit on top of the pudding mixture, and a larger circle of greaseproof paper to cover the whole basin top like a lid. Finally, cover each basin with a cloth and tie it down with string.

Stand the puddings in pans containing enough water to come halfway up the side of each basin, put a tight-fitting lid on each pan, and steam over a low heat for 3 hours. Make sure the water in the pans does not dry out, by topping it up every 30–40 minutes with boiling water from the kettle (cold water will bring the temperature down).

Leave the puddings to cool, then hide them away to mature in a dark cool cupboard for a minimum of 1 month. I like to leave them for about 3 months, and a year is really good. Any longer becomes questionable, but in theory is great! Surprising as it sounds, the puddings will keep for a year as long as they are left untouched after cooking. I tend to eat one and leave the other alone until you want to use it later, or the following year. The third I give away to someone as a gift.

On the day you want to eat the pudding, steam it slowly in a pan with hot water halfway up the sides for 1½ hours, until heated through. Once it's cooked, I turn out the pudding, prick holes in it, then pour brandy over and set it on fire with a match at the table.

Here are some tips for firing up your pudding:

✳ When steaming, wrap the pudding tightly in greaseproof paper and foil, so that no water can get in while it's reheating.

✳ Turn the pudding out by putting a plate on top and flipping it over.

✳ Before lighting the pudding, clear the surrounding area.

✳ Gently warm the brandy in a small saucepan or ladle before lighting, to achieve a bigger flame.

✳ Tip the brandy to the side of the pan or ladle before lighting.

✳ Point the pan or ladle away from you when pouring the lit brandy over the pudding.

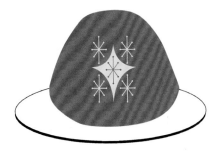

CHEESE PLATE

I've called on my favourite cheese guys from Raw Cheese Power to help me devise the perfect cheese plate. The trick is to find a balance between sharing and self-indulgence. You can go for four basic categories: soft, medium, hard and blue.

BUYING

There are no rules. We're all different. Have fun. Explore. Experiment. Discover. The same goes for pairings; try cider and beer as well as wine and fizz. Match the sweetness of a grape with the saltiness of a Stilton. Try a sharp Cheshire with apple pie, or Cheddar with a strong porter beer.

STORING

Serve above 15°C (59°F), certainly not straight out of the fridge. Let it get it oozy and stinky. Treat it like a wine, and let it breathe before consuming. To store, wrap the cheeses individually in cheese (waxed) paper so air and moisture can't wreck them. It's recommended to keep different types of cheese, such as white bloomy rinds, blues and hard cheeses, separate. (This is especially the case for washed rind cheeses, as the scent can taint all the less robust varieties.) If storing in plastic containers as well, refresh the air everyday, let the cheeses breathe, then rewrap.

Soft and blue cheeses should be stored at 4–8°C (39–46°F).

Semi-hard and hard cheeses should be stored at 8–12°C (46–53°F).

ARRANGING

Buy some classic crowd-pleasers if you're sharing and select a few cheeses that people might not know to make an interesting selection. Mix them up for taste and texture. I make sure I allow a flow from the softer and gooiest cheeses to the hardest...

Gooey: Brie, St Marcelin, Gorgonzola.

Lactic, mild & tangy: Fresh goats' cheese such as Clifton Leaf or Rouelle du Tarn.

Sour & crumbly: Wensleydale, Bourne's Cheshire, or ewes' milk Swaledale.

Sticky, stinky rind-washed: My personal favourite category, I like Aged Abondance or Jumi's Aarewasser.

Rich intense goat: There are a lot to choose from, I've recently discovered Tor from Glastonbury, which is based on the classic French Loire Valley goats' cheeses.

Hard: Cheddar is unbeatable. I like Barbers vintage and aged Lincolnshire Poacher. You could also try Gruyère, Gouda, Comté, or Grana Padano.

Blue: It's Christmas, so you've got to have some Stilton – I love Colston Bassett which is crumbly, creamy, chocolatey with salt. BUT... explore the world of the blues. There are literally hundreds.

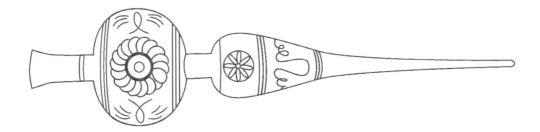

BREAD OR CRACKERS?

Both for me. It's Christmas, so why not push the boat out? I prefer to pair cheese with heritage grain sourdough bread and a selection of crackers. The roughness of the grain is brilliant with cheese. I also love fruit and nut sourdough breads. These are both artisan and can be sourced from specialist bakers. A good baguette, preferably sourdough, is a winner too. As it's Christmas, leftover Christmas cake is a brilliant accompaniment, but if you've never tried cheese with malt loaf you are missing out!

SERVING SUGGESTIONS

Frozen grapes: Bung a bunch of red or black grapes in the freezer overnight and whip them out just before you're ready to serve your cheese plate; they go really sparkly and the icy cold texture is a revelation with cheese.

Dehydrated grapes: Place a bunch of red, white or black grapes on to a baking tray and bake in a preheated oven at 50°C (122°F), or the lowest temperature your oven will go, for 12 hours or overnight. In the morning they will be shriveled up like extra-juicy raisins which, once cool, are terrific with cheese.

Fresh grapes: Alternatively don't mess about with grapes at all and serve your cheese the classic way with a bunch of fresh grapes.

Fresh slices of pear or apple: One of the simplest, best accompaniments with most cheeses.

Fresh figs: These go well with the rind-washed or goats' cheeses.

Celery sticks: Brilliant with hard cheeses.

Pickled fruits and nuts: I love to serve cheese alongside pickled fruits, such as my Quickest Pickled Pineapple (see page 107) or pickled pears. Mustard fruits, quince and pickled walnuts are my other favourites.

Chutneys: Serving chutneys from spoons is a really cool way to show them off. I love a good quince, pear or dried fruit chutney at Christmas.

The festive holidays are a time of decadence and overindulgence, and quite rightly so! However, I think it's so important to avoid letting this glut of food go to waste – not just for ethical reasons, but also because otherwise you miss out on so much deliciousness!

Every household that cooks a turkey or any other large bird is guaranteed to have a load of meat left on the bird. There is nothing worse than allowing a dried-out carcass to take over your fridge, so once you've recovered from the main meal, pick the bird for every last scrap of meat. If you're anything like me, you'll have a craving for chilli to zing your taste buds back into action. So I've included two great recipes that do just that, my Infamous Erskine Turkey Curry and a Mexican twist with Turkey Mole Enchiladas. My favourite thing of all time is the French Dip Leftover Sandwich, where you pile ALL OF CHRISTMAS into a sandwich and plunge it into hot gravy. I'm basically obsessed with gravy, and this takes the boring old leftover sandwich to the next level.

There are so many dishes you can make from leftovers, from using bones to make simple stocks and nourishing soups, to throwing leftover veg into a pan and making the ultimate Bubble & Squeak. That's my December 27th dish. I take my niece and nephew to the pantomime, then afterwards we go home for a heaping pile of bubble with roast ham and pickles. My sister has lost her mind in the past when I've gone out for the day and she's had to wait 'til late to have this.

This time of year is always when family start to disperse and mates are involved. It's that brilliant time of respite when you've kind of had enough and want some normal chat BUT want it to still feel festive. I'm writing this and feeling just as excited about the idea of what you can do with all the leftover food as I am about Christmas itself. Leftover recipes have now become an important "tradition" to me, so I think it's fair to say that what is sometimes seen as second best is now a very important star of the show.

Festive
foraging

TURKEY MOLE ENCHILADAS

While the spiciness and fresh accompaniments here are a welcome break from any heavy foods, there is something reassuringly comforting in the spices and the cocoa. This recipe is terrific for using up leftover turkey, but you could also poach a whole chicken to make it.

500g (1lb 2oz) tomatoes

1–2 tablespoons rapeseed
or olive oil

1 large onion, finely chopped

6 garlic cloves, finely chopped

a few thyme sprigs

50g (1¾oz) ground almonds

2 tablespoons ground cumin

1 teaspoon chilli powder

½ teaspoon ground cinnamon

¼ teaspoon ground cloves

a pinch of freshly grated nutmeg

1–2 teaspoons cocoa powder

700ml (1¼ pints) fresh chicken stock

400g (14oz) leftover cooked turkey
or chicken, shredded

4 medium or 8 small corn tortillas

120g (4¼oz) Cheddar cheese, grated
plus 30g (1oz) extra for topping

To serve

2 avocados

juice of 3 limes

sea salt flakes

4 tomatoes, chopped

1 red chilli, finely chopped

1 garlic clove, finely grated

100g (3½oz) soured cream

1 Little Gem lettuce, finely shredded

3 tablespoons pickled jalapeño chillies,
drained

half a small bunch (about 15g/½oz)
fresh coriander

Before you start you need to char your tomatoes. You can do this one of two ways: the "safe" way, by roasting them at the highest temperature your oven goes until the skins just blacken, or the more risky way of charring them on a griddle pan or over an actual flame. The charring adds flavour, so once blackened, bung the tomatoes, skins and all, into a blender and blitz until puréed.

Heat the oil in a medium saucepan and fry the onion very slowly over a medium heat for 10–15 minutes, or until the onion has fully softened and started to turn golden brown. Add the garlic and thyme for the last couple of minutes of cooking. Now turn up the heat, add the ground almonds, and toast them for a couple of minutes. Add the spices and the cocoa powder and cook for a minute, then add the puréed tomatoes. They will be quite liquidy, so you will need to cook them until they have dried out a little, to concentrate the tomato flavour. Add the stock to the pan and cook for 20 minutes, or until the sauce has begun to thicken, reduce and become rich and full-flavoured.

Preheat the oven to 220°C/200°C fan (425°F), Gas Mark 7. Put the sauce into a blender and blitz until smooth. Pour three-quarters of the sauce back into the pan, along with your shredded turkey or chicken meat, and cook slowly over a low heat for a further 15 minutes. (The rest of the sauce will be used to top the enchiladas.) As it cooks the meat will get really "shreddy" now, and the sauce will get very intense in flavour.

In a dry frying pan, quickly warm your tortillas over a high heat. Divide the filling and the grated cheese between the tortillas and roll them up like cannelloni, placing them neatly in a row into a 2-litre (3½ pint) baking dish. Pour over the reserved sauce and top with the remaining cheese. Bake in the oven for 20 minutes, or until the cheese has melted and the dish is bubbling and golden.

Meanwhile chop the avocados and mix with the juice of 2 of the limes and salt to taste. In a separate bowl, mix the chopped tomatoes with the chilli, garlic, remaining lime juice and salt to taste. Serve the enchiladas with the chopped avocado, salsa, soured cream, lettuce, jalapeños and coriander.

THE INFAMOUS ERSKINE TURKEY CURRY

Christmas lunch is always turkey for me, not through lack of trying to get other birds on the menu, but because my sisters just won't budge towards goose or duck. This is no great pity, as I love turkey for Christmas lunch and I love turkey sandwiches on Christmas night for supper, but what I really love is the Erskine family's world-famous turkey curry (see photograph on pages 212–3). It has hints of the Thai influences my family was bought up with. I think it's now time it was passed on.

3 tablespoons vegetable oil

2 onions, finely chopped

3–4 garlic cloves, chopped

3cm (1¼ inch) piece of fresh root ginger, finely grated

1 tablespoon ground cumin

½ tablespoon ground coriander

½ teaspoon chilli powder

½ teaspoon garam masala

a pinch of ground cloves

1 cinnamon stick

½ teaspoon ground turmeric

1 bay leaf

½ tablespoon plain flour

400ml (14fl oz) fresh chicken stock, or leftover turkey gravy

600g (1lb 5oz) leftover cooked turkey, chopped or shredded into bite-sized pieces

1 teaspoon brown or palm sugar

1 tablespoon fish sauce

100ml (3½oz) coconut cream, plus more to serve

6 shallots, thinly sliced

fresh coriander leaves, to serve

Thai basil leaves (optional; in the unlikey event you have these knocking about, they garnish the curry brilliantly)

cooked basmati rice, to serve

Heat 2 tablespoons of the oil in a large pan and gently fry the onions for 15 minutes, or until they have softened and are tinged golden. Add the garlic and ginger and cook for a further minute. Stir in the spices, bay leaf (and the flour if using stock; you won't need it if you're using gravy) and cook for 30 seconds, then pour over the chicken stock or turkey gravy. Add the chopped or shredded turkey.

Once the curry starts to bubble, reduce the temperature to a slow simmer and add the sugar, fish sauce and coconut cream. Cook for 20 minutes, until the flavours have emulsified and the curry looks rich.

Meanwhile, heat the remaining vegetable oil in a small frying pan and fry the shallots slowly over a low heat until crisp. Drain on kitchen paper.

Check the seasoning of the curry, then serve with plain basmati rice. Top each portion of curry with the crispy shallots, more coconut cream and lots of fresh coriander and Thai basil leaves (if using).

MY FRENCH DIP CHRISTMAS LEFTOVER SANDWICH

This is without doubt the best sandwich known to man. You've got the fillings, so I urge you to give it a go. I put EVERYTHING into it, but obviously only use the ingredients you really fancy and serve it hot or cold. The essential thing is the hot leftover gravy to plunge the sandwich of dreams into! For true Christmas gluttony I serve this alongside cheese, a slice of pork pie, ham and loads of pickles and chutneys.

50ml (2fl oz) leftover gravy
  (per person)

2 slices of proper white chewy bread

butter, for spreading

1 tablespoon mayonnaise, freshly
  made or bought (either is fine)

1 tablespoon cranberry sauce

2–3 slices of leftover cooked turkey

2 tablespoons leftover stuffing

1 pig in blanket, sliced into
  4 lengthways

1 tablespoon bread sauce

2 lettuce leaves (I use Little Gems),
  shredded

Before you make your sandwich, reheat the gravy until it's piping hot. Butter the bread on one side, then spread the mayo on one slice and the cranberry sauce on the other. Lay the turkey on the cranberry side, topped with the stuffing, which you can flatten out with the back of a spoon.

Top with the sliced pig in blanket, then the bread sauce, and finally the salad, and seal with the mayo-ed slice of bread. Cut in half and dip into the gravy with each bite...

SWEET POTATO, SPROUT & SWEETCORN HASH

When testing recipes for this book I had an abundance of fantastic ingredients left over, and while one of the great things is working with seasonal ingredients, naturally when doing my kind of job you still have too much food. This led me to invent this breakfast dish by complete accident. I took what I had left in the fridge and just bunged it into a pan to make the most phenomenal (and, as it happens, very healthy) hash. It's now one of my favourite breakfasts. It takes 15 minutes, and because of the amount of natural sugars, fats and protein, it may be the perfect healthy hangover cure...

1 sweet potato, peeled (if you like) and chopped into 1.5cm (⅝ inch) cubes

10 Brussels sprouts, trimmed and shredded

1 sweetcorn cob, stripped of its kernels

3 tablespoons cold pressed rapeseed oil

juice of 1–2 limes, plus lime wedges to serve

small bunch (about 15g/½oz) of fresh coriander, roughly chopped

2 really good-quality free-range eggs (I use Cotswold Legbars or Burford Browns for their orange yolks, or even duck eggs)

1 avocado, peeled, halved and sliced

whatever hot sauce you like, to serve

sea salt flakes and freshly ground black pepper

Find a deep frying pan, one that can be covered with a large lid. Place the sweet potato, sprouts and corn in the pan with a decent splash of water (about 1½ tablespoons) and 1 tablespoon of the oil. Pop the pan on the hob and cover with the lid. Increase the heat to its highest until the water is boiling, then reduce the temperature to allow the veg to steam for 3–4 minutes, or until the water has evaporated. You can give it all a stir halfway through to make sure nothing is sticking. The veg should be becoming tender, but won't be cooked through yet.

Remove the lid and increase the heat again. Now the water has evaporated you want to fry the mixture. Stir-fry for 8–10 minutes, or until the veg is cooked through and a little charred on the outside. Season well with salt and pepper and stir in half the lime juice (to taste) and the coriander. Plate up the hash, then fry the eggs in the rest of the oil. Pop the eggs on top of the hash and serve with the sliced avocado, doused with the remaining lime juice, and some salt. Finally, hot sauce that baby up! If you're feeling delicate, you will be back together in no time!

THAI GOOSE, BUTTERNUT SQUASH & POMEGRANATE SALAD

After a mammoth amount of heavy food, a salad is a welcome respite. In this recipe, leftover goose is crisped-up in the oven in goose fat and hoisin sauce, then mixed with a salad of spiced and roasted butternut squash, pomegranate and a mega amount of fresh herbs, all brought together in a zingy Thai dressing. You can do this with turkey too, but when the goose fat renders down it goes extra crispy and makes for the most BRILLIANT flavour and texture combo.

600g (1lb 5oz) butternut squash, peeled and cut into 12 wedges

1 tablespoon olive oil

½ teaspoon ground cinnamon

1 teaspoon chilli flakes

550g (1lb 4oz) leftover cooked goose, including the skin

2 tablespoons goose fat

4 tablespoons best-quality hoisin sauce (I like the Flying Goose brand, ironically)

8 shallots, finely sliced

1 tablespoon vegetable oil

a large bunch of Thai basil

a small bunch each of coriander and mint

100g (3½oz) pomegranate seeds

100g (3½oz) cashew nuts, toasted

sea salt flakes and freshly ground black pepper

For the dressing

juice of 3 limes

juice of 1 mandarin

3 tablespoons brown sugar

3 tablespoons fish sauce

1 garlic clove, finely grated

3cm (1¼ inch) piece of fresh root ginger, finely grated

1–2 Thai red chillies, seeds in or out

Heat the oven to 220°C/200°C fan (425°F), Gas Mark 7. Put the butternut squash into a roasting pan and toss with the tablespoon of olive oil, cinnamon and chilli flakes. Season with salt and pepper. Roast for 25 minutes, until soft but still retaining a little bite. Remove from the roasting pan and leave aside to cool.

Now add the goose to the same pan, and spread with the goose fat. Season with salt and pepper and put into the oven. After 15 minutes, remove and stir in the hoisin sauce. Return to the oven for a further 10 minutes, stirring a couple of times as it cooks. Remove from the oven when the goose is nicely caramelized and crispy.

Meanwhile, take two-thirds of the sliced shallots and fry in the vegetable oil over a low heat for 10–15 minutes or until they start to crisp up and turn a light golden colour. Scoop out and drain on kitchen paper.

To make the dressing, put all the ingredients into a small food processor or use a mortar and pestle and whizz or bash together until blended.

Now you are ready to construct the salad. Pick the leaves from all the herbs and put into a large bowl. Add the squash, pomegranate seeds, cashews, remaining raw shallots and the dressing. Mix thoroughly, then throw in the goose and give another good mix. Plate up, and sprinkle over the crispy shallots before serving. Hey presto! You have one mean salad to lighten up the Christmas load.

BUBBLE & SQUEAK

* SERVES 4–6, DEPENDING ON WHAT YOU'RE SERVING IT WITH
* PREPARATION TIME: 15 MINUTES
* COOKING TIME: 20 MINUTES

I'm not sure this even needs a recipe, but the standard vegetable mash-up just has to be included in this book. My family would go crackers if we didn't have it. I make mine only with leftover veg, but I know some people love bunging stuffing and leftover pigs in blankets in there too. And we serve ours with ham and pickles, my favourite being a whole slice of Quickest Pickled Pineapple (see page 107).

2 tablespoons olive oil

1 tablespoon unsalted butter

approximately 1kg (2lb 4oz) leftover vegetables from your roast lunch (50% should be potatoes and parsnips, the rest carrots, sprouts, peas, cabbage – everything but beetroot and red cabbage), roughly chopped

Find yourself a large good non-stick frying pan – I do favour using a non-stick for this unless you're some kind of Spanish tortilla expert. Heat the fats until they are foaming, then pile the vegetables into the pan. Stir-fry for a minute or so. This will start to soften them again, but will also get them evenly mixed.

You can use the back of the spoon to start squashing the veg so it makes a really rough mash, working everything together in the pan and pushing it down so that the mixture covers the base – allow the mixture to brown slightly on the bottom before flipping the mixture over and doing the same again. It's the bits of potato that catch in the pan that define the term 'bubble and squeak', so be brave and let the mixture colour. Some people like to turn it out like a frittata and cut it into wedges, but I prefer to scoop it out old-fashioned style.

FRIED CHRISTMAS PUDDING

* SERVES 2
* PREPARATION TIME: 5 MINUTES
* COOKING TIME: 5 MINUTES

This is not really a recipe, but a way to eat Christmas pudding (there are three ways... this is no. 1. No. 2 is flamed on the Christmas table and no. 3 is with some Stilton sliced on top, like a really good fruit bread). You can also use a traditional fruit Christmas cake. Fried in butter until crisp, then slathered with pouring cream. It has to be pouring cream – none of this fancy boozy nonsense!

2 tablespoons unsalted butter

slices of leftover Christmas pudding, 2cm (¾ inch) thick

pouring cream

Heat the butter in a heavy-bottomed frying pan until it starts to foam. Lay the sliced Christmas pudding in the pan and fry for a couple of minutes over a medium heat, until the bottom of the pudding has crisped up, then flip it over and fry until crisp on the other side. Serve on small pudding plates, with pouring cream.

So, you've spent the festive period eating and drinking until you're full to bursting. New Year's Eve is the final chance for celebration before we spend the rest of January full of guilt and good intentions – the final furlong! So whether you are thinking of hosting a party, holding a more civilised sit-down meal, or are just looking for something delicious to line your stomach with before you go out on the town, there is a recipe here for you. I haven't included anything too fussy, as you may have spent long enough in the kitchen over the festive period, but here you'll find a REALLY good flavoursome chicken stew and a Tartiflette as well as my dream hangover cure, Breakfast Carbonara, and, to head us off into the New Year with the best of the European traditions, Galette des Rois.

Hogmanay has its roots in Viking traditions, brought over after their invasion and settlement in Scotland and Northern England in the 8th and 9th centuries. The marking of the winter solstice was an extremely important festival for the Vikings. I hadn't realized that Christmas was effectively banned in Scotland after the Protestant reformation in the late 17th century right up until the 1950s, so New Year became the main focus for celebration. There are lots of traditions connected to Hogmanay, for example that of "First Footing". Historically this is the custom intended to encourage good luck for the rest of the year. After the strike of midnight, the household would wait for the first person to cross the threshold, ideally a man with dark hair bearing gifts of coal, shortbread, a silver coin and perhaps some foliage.

The coal would represent a warm house for the coming year, shortbread to ensure the family is fed, silver for wealth and greenery to symbolise a long life. The guest would then leave with the ashes of the fire to signify the departure of the old year. The origins of the wish for a dark haired man to enter probably stems from the Viking invasion, when blonde haired strangers arriving at your doorstep more often than not meant trouble!

Auld Lang Syne is a song that is sung across the Western World on New Year's Eve, translating from the Scottish Gaelic as "time's gone by", first made famous when Robert Burns published it in 1796. However, the song as we know it today wasn't popularised until the late 1920s, when Canadian Guy Lombardo heard Scottish immigrants singing it in his hometown of London, Ontario. To this day his recording is still the first song played after the strike of midnight in Times Square in New York.

Loud noise making, fireworks and parades are found in all cultures around the world at the turn of the year, thought to help dispel evil spirits and bring good luck, while bringing light to the darkness in the depths of winter – see my tips on how to enjoy fireworks. Likewise, the tradition of making resolutions is held all over the world, believed to date back as far as the Babylonians! I hope I am not alone in consistently making and breaking my resolutions, but I do see the beginning of the year as an opportunity to reflect on what's past, and put out good energy and wishes for the future. Happy New Year!

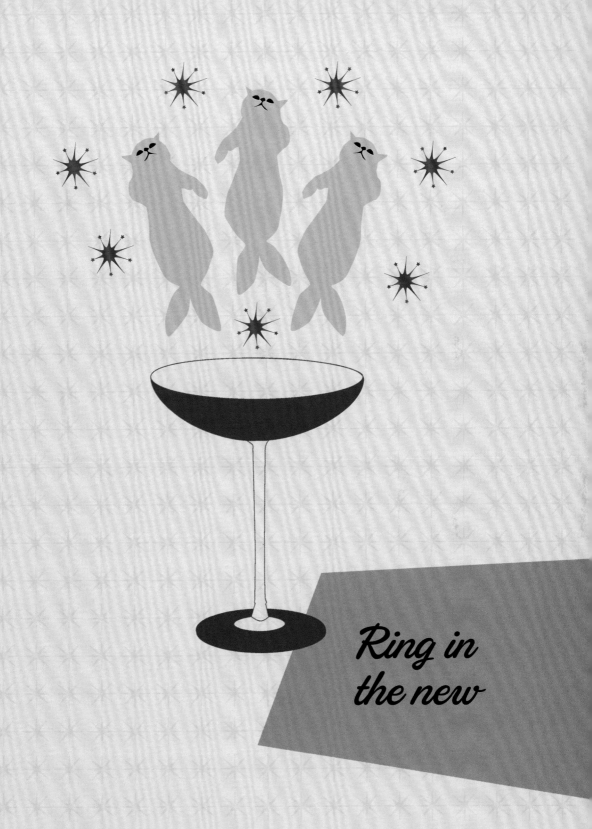

Ring in
the new

FRIJOLES
WITH SWEET POTATO SKINS

I spent New Year's Eve in America last year, and when I asked what people ate, most of them said a big vat of stewed beans, while the others said a roast rib of beef. So here we have a vat of *frijoles*, which are black beans stewed with spices. I've kept this recipe vegetarian, but if you are happy to use proper chicken stock, it will increase the flavour since this is normally made with a big pork, ham bone or chicken carcass. I've served it with sweet potato wedges, avocado, soured cream and jalapeños. It's a super-easy one-pot dish, and any leftovers make the most terrific breakfast with Gooey Sweetcorn Cakes (see page 226).

2 sweet potatoes

2 tablespoons olive oil, plus extra for the sweet potatoes

1 garlic bulb, cut in half horizontally

2 onions, finely chopped

1 tablespoon ground cumin

1 tablespoon ground coriander

2 x 400g (14oz) cans of black beans (keep the liquid)

400ml (14fl oz) fresh vegetable or chicken stock

1 bay leaf

a few thyme sprigs, leaves picked

2 ripe avocados

juice of ½ lemon

4 tablespoons soured cream

100g (3½oz) feta cheese

a small bunch of coriander, roughly chopped

sea salt flakes and freshly ground black pepper

Preheat your oven to 200°C/180°C fan (400°F), Gas Mark 6. Place your sweet potatoes on a baking tray and bake for 50 minutes.

Meanwhile, heat the oil in a large saucepan, add the garlic, flat side-down, and let it caramelize for a minute or so. Remove from the pan and set aside. Next add the onions and soften over a medium to low heat for 10–15 minutes, adding the garlic back for the last couple of minutes. Add the spices and fry for a further 2 minutes, then add the beans (including their liquid), the stock, bay leaf and thyme. Season with a little salt and pepper and cook over a medium to low heat for 30 minutes. It should be really stewy, almost soupy.

Once the sweet potatoes are cooked, remove from the oven and ramp up the oven temperature as high as it will go. Leave the potatoes to cool for a few minutes, then cut in half lengthways. Scoop out most of the flesh but avoid scooping all the way down to the skins – you want to form little boats that are perfect for dipping and scooping up the beans. Drizzle with olive oil and return to the oven for about 15 minutes to crisp up a little. Meanwhile, stir the potato flesh into the stew.

Just before serving, peel and stone the avocados, then slice the flesh and sprinkle with a little lemon juice and salt. Serve the beans with the sweet potato boats, sliced avocado, a tablespoon of soured cream, a crumbling of feta, and a small handful of coriander.

LEFTOVER PAKORAS

✳ SERVES 4–6
✳ PREPARATION TIME: 15 MINUTES
✳ COOKING TIME: 15 MINUTES

It's pretty hard to transform leftover vegetables into anything but bubble and squeak, but if you wanted to try something a little less basic that you could use to entertain unexpected guests, make these. They're spicy, aromatic and crispy and take minutes to fry up. You need to use gram flour for flavour and to get that real crispiness – nothing else will do I'm afraid, but it's worth having some about the house anyway, as we're seeing it used in more and more recipes these days. I serve these with a lime pickle and yogurt, which is a lively combination of sour, spicy, salty and creamy, but I've been known to have a little mango or date chutney on the side too.

100g (3½oz) gram (chickpea) flour

1 teaspoon sea salt flakes

2 teaspoons garam masala

1 teaspoon ground turmeric

1 teaspoon cumin seeds

½ teaspoon red chilli powder

2 green chillies, finely chopped

1 tablespoon finely grated fresh root ginger (optional)

a handful of coriander, finely chopped

2 teaspoons dried fenugreek leaves

1 onion, thinly sliced

4–6 leftover roast potatoes, roughly chopped

10 leftover cooked Brussels sprouts, quartered

2 leftover cooked carrots, roughly chopped

1 leftover cooked parsnip, roughly chopped

50g (1¾oz) frozen peas

oil, for deep-frying

Mix the gram flour with enough water to bring it together to a thick paste, a bit like a thick waffle batter. Add the salt and spices, the chillies, ginger, coriander and fenugreek and get them really well combined. If you have time, let the batter rest for 1 hour in the fridge. It will be really super-crisp if it goes cold into hot fat, and also resting gives time for all the flavours to come together; however, you can use it straight away if you like.

Stir in all the veg. They should be somewhere between being coated and swimming in the batter. You can cook them in a deep-fat fryer at 180°C (350°F), but I like to pour oil into a deep frying pan, saucepan or wok, making sure the fat only comes one-third of the way up the side of the pan. Get the oil nice and hot. If you have a thermometer, it needs to reach 180°C (350°F), but if not, simply wait until a drop of the batter put into the oil sizzles pleasingly.

When you're all set, carefully dollop large spoonfuls of the battered vegetables in batches into the oil and fry on both sides for 2–3 minutes, until crisp and cooked through. Scoop out of the oil with a slotted spoon and place on a plate topped with plenty of kitchen paper, then sprinkle with salt. Repeat until all the pakoras are fried – you can keep previous batches warm in a low oven while you do this.

GOOEY CHEESY-MIDDLE SWEETCORN CAKES
WITH AVOCADO, EGGS & SALSA

These are not your conventional sweetcorn cakes like the Australian or Thai style with whole bits of corn in them. These are somewhere between an *arepa* (a Columbian corn cake that's been stuffed) and a fluffy pancake, but made with fresh corn and polenta. I'm serving them here with fried eggs, avocado and tomato salsa, but if you've made the Frijoles (see page 222) the night before and have any left over, a scoop of that alongside makes a mighty great brunch.

100g (3½oz) fresh or frozen sweetcorn kernels

100g (3½oz) fine polenta meal (I like the stuff used for making corn tortillas)

100ml (3½fl oz) milk

1 free-range egg, plus 2 or 4 extra (depending on how hungry you are)

1 teaspoon baking powder

vegetable or rapeseed oil, for frying

1 small ball of mozzarella, finely chopped

1 ripe but firm avocado

juice of ½ lemon

sprigs of coriander, for serving

70g (2½oz) feta cheese, crumbled

leftover Frijoles (see page 222, optional)

sea salt flakes

For the salsa

3–4 tomatoes, deseeded and roughly chopped

1 red chilli, deseeded and finely chopped

a decent dash of your favourite chilli sauce, to taste

1 garlic clove, finely grated

the juice of 1 really juicy lime

½ tablespoon extra virgin olive oil

To make the pancakes, place the corn, polenta, milk, 1 egg, the baking powder and a pinch of salt in a food processor and blitz until combined and the corn kernels have broken up but still have some texture.

Meanwhile, mix all the salsa ingredients together until well combined. Set aside.

To make the pancakes, heat a frying pan or pancake pan over a low to medium heat. Wipe the base of the pan with a little bit of oil. Now, you can do this in 2 ways. You can dollop the mixture in using a spoon or ladle, but personally I prefer using 8cm (3¼ in) cooking rings or crumpet moulds: oil the rings and place in the pan. Spoon 1–2 tablespoons of the sweetcorn mixture into the rings to form a base, sprinkle with a quarter of the mozzarella, then top with another 1–2 tablespoons of the sweetcorn mixture. Cook over a medium to low heat for 3–4 minutes, then carefully ease the cakes out of the rings and flip them over to finish cooking on the other side for another 2–3 minutes. They should be golden on each side, cooked through but with gooey cheese in the middle. The mixture will make 4 cakes and you can keep them warm in a low-ish oven, about 140°C/120°C fan (275°F), Gas Mark 1, for a maximum of 10 minutes.

Peel and stone the avocado, then chop the flesh and sprinkle with a little lemon juice and salt.

Fry the eggs to your liking (for me I need a runny yolk), then serve 2 cakes per person with the fried eggs, the sliced and dressed avocado, the salsa, coriander, crumbled feta and Frijoles, if you like.

TARTIFLETTE DE SAVOYARD-(ISH)

Cheese, bacon, potatoes, sweet sticky onions, cream... What's not to love? Tartiflette is an Alpine dish made with all these wonderful ingredients, baked slowly together as a traybake until the potatoes are soft and surrounded by a wicked cheesy cream sauce studded with bacon. It makes the most brilliant dinner party dish, especially for a New Year's soirée, as it's elegant but still very simple. If I'm entertaining I want to not have to think about doing too much work, so I can focus on being a good host. The "ish" comes into the name because my version is not completely classic. You can use Vacherin, which is a little easier to get hold of than the traditional Reblochon, and I've also grated Gruyère over the top and made it a little more refined like a buxom dauphinoise (see photograph on page 227). This is served simply with plenty of good wine, some cornichons and pickled white onions, and a crisp green salad.

4 tablespoons olive oil

400g thick-sliced smoked streaky bacon, cut into thin strips or lardons

2 garlic cloves, thinly sliced

4 onions, thinly sliced

a few thyme sprigs

1kg (2lb 4oz) potatoes (ones that hold their shape but aren't particularly "waxy" – I like Maris Piper)

1 small glass of white wine

100ml (3½fl oz) whole milk

300ml (10fl oz) crème fraiche

a good pinch of freshly grated nutmeg

1 whole ripe Reblochon or Vacherin cheese

30g (1oz) Gruyère cheese, grated

sea salt flakes and freshly ground black pepper

To serve

salad leaves

cornichons

white pickled onions

Heat the oven to 190°C/170°C fan (375°F), Gas Mark 5. Heat 2 tablespoons of the oil in a medium casserole pan. Add the bacon and fry until golden and starting to crisp, adding the garlic for the last minute of cooking. Remove with a slotted spoon and set aside. Add the rest of the oil to the pan and throw in the onions and thyme. Fry over a medium heat for 5 minutes, then reduce the heat and cook very slowly for a further 25–35 minutes. What you're wanting is close to an onion jam consistency. Really sweet, only just caramelized onions. This does take gentle cooking, but it's worth every second. When they're done, put the bacon back into the pan.

Next up, slice your potatoes. I would use a mandolin, which is a chef's slicing tool, but you can do it by hand or in a food processor fitted with the slicing blade. Traditionally the potatoes are thickly sliced – I like them a little thinner and more "refined", but you can cut them however you feel comfortable.

Put a layer of the sliced potatoes in the bottom of an ovenproof dish, and sprinkle over some of the onion, bacon and garlic mix to make another layer. Season with salt and pepper (easy on the salt, as the bacon and cheese are salty already).

Add another layer of potato, top again with bacon and onion, and season. Keep going until you've used everything up. Mix together the wine, milk and crème fraiche and season with plenty of black pepper, some nutmeg and a little salt, bearing in mind that the cheese is very salty. Pour this over the potatoes. There should be just enough so everything is lapping up the juice.

Cut the Reblochon or Vacherin cheese horizontally in half. These cheeses can both be quite sticky, so using a hot knife is best. (Remember, a Vacherin has an extra layer of wooden casing, so to stop it oozing everywhere gently carve this out.) Classically you would plonk the rounds of cheese face down on to the top of the bake, but I'm a neat freak and from a family of three greedy girls, so I like each portion to be fair: I like the whole dish to be covered with the cheese, so I now cut each half into 3, so you have 6 slices of cheese. Lay these cut sides down on top of the bake and push down hard so the cheese sits in the sauce. Sprinkle with the Gruyère.

Bake for 50 minutes, or until the cheese is bubbling and golden, maybe a little bit scorchy, and the potatoes are cooked through. Keep an eye on the top, as it may need covering with foil so that it doesn't burn or get too brown. Serve with salad, cornichons, pickled white onions and PLENTY of wine...

SERVES 6

PREPARATION TIME: 30 MINUTES

COOKING TIME: 2 HOURS

CHICKEN, CHORIZO & SPELT CASSEROLE

One-pot dishes don't usually have an elegant finish to them, but some recipes manage to just preach buxom flavour in only a few stages. This is a kind of in-your-face flavour but with a snazzy overtone. It is a rich casserole made with chicken and chorizo sausages but filled out with pearled spelt, which, like a stewy rice dish such as a paella, sucks up all the flavour. Finished with a heightened tang from lemon zest and parsley, it's the kind of food people (or at least I) live for – all made in one pot!

2 tablespoons olive oil

1 large free-range chicken, jointed into 10 pieces (you can ask your butcher to do this)

6 small whole cooking chorizos, about 340g (11¾oz)

1 large garlic bulb, cut in half horizontally

2 onions, finely chopped

1 bottle of dry white wine

800ml (1⅓ pints) fresh chicken stock, plus extra if needed

a generous pinch of saffron

2 bay leaves

1 rosemary sprig

a few thyme sprigs, leaves picked

a small bunch of flat-leaf parsley, leaves chopped

300g (10½oz) pearled spelt

finely grated zest of 1 lemon

sea salt flakes and freshly ground black pepper

Preheat the oven to 220°C/200°C fan (425°F), Gas Mark 7. Heat the oil in a large ovenproof casserole dish. Season the chicken pieces with salt and put them into the dish, pressing them firmly skin side down. Brown thoroughly in batches, until you achieve a lovely deep caramel colour – this will create a great depth of flavour. Once the chicken is browned, remove with tongs and set aside.

Brown the chorizos all over in the same dish, then remove and set aside. Next lay the garlic bulb halves in the dish, cut sides down, and let them caramelize for1 minute, but be careful not to let them burn, as this will create a bitter flavour. Remove and set aside.

Add your chopped onions to the residual oil in the pan and fry them slowly for 10–12 minutes, until they start to soften. Pour over the wine and chicken stock, add the saffron, bay leaves, rosemary, thyme and half the parsley, and bring to the boil. Add the chicken, garlic, chorizo and spelt to the casserole. The chicken needs to be 90 per cent covered with liquid, so top it up with a little more stock if necessary. Place the lid on the dish and transfer to the oven. Cook for 15 minutes, then reduce the temperature to 200°C/180°C fan (400°F), Gas Mark 6 and cook for a further 45 minutes.

Once the time's up, remove from the oven and leave to rest for 5–10 minutes. Stir through the remaining parsley and the lemon zest and serve with a salad.

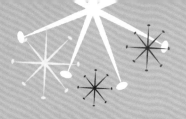

New Year firework
TIPS

It's easy to get caught up in the excitement of firework events, so here are a few simple tips to ensure your night goes off with the right kind of bang!

✳ Unless you are lucky enough to have a large garden, I wouldn't recommend organizing a firework display of your own. There are so many good professional events, and they are safer and more eco-friendly.

✳ Sparklers are among the biggest cause of injuries among children at firework events, so make sure any little ones have proper adult supervision. Sparklers are not recommended for children under 5.

✳ It's a good idea to make sure gloves are worn when handling sparklers, to help protect against burns. Make sure sparklers are held at arm's length away from the body.

✳ Only light one sparkler at a time, and avoid standing anywhere windy.

✳ Place any used sparklers in a bucket of water, as the ends are still hot even when they've gone out.

✳ Fireworks can be a bit of a nightmare if you have a house full of animals like I do. I get a mixed response. Both my cats sit at the window to watch, while the dog hides under the bed quivering. You could invest in a room diffuser specifically designed to help calm animals (I use Feliway).

✳ It's a good idea to make sure to take any dogs for a walk before it gets dark and before fireworks are likely to begin. Keep cats indoors and don't take dogs to fireworks displays. Shut windows and close curtains to reduce noise, and make sure the house is secure and there's no way for your animals to escape if they get scared and want to run away. On that note, make sure that all pets are microchipped in case they do run off.

✳ If you are lighting a few fireworks yourself, this is a job for (sober) grown-ups.

✳ Ensure any fireworks you buy are intended for home/consumer use.

✳ Store any fireworks in a dry, metal box, such as a biscuit tin.

✳ Use a long taper to light fireworks, rather than a lighter or small match.

✳ Make sure there is nothing flammable in the surrounding area where you are lighting the fireworks.

✳ Make sure fireworks are legal in your area before using them. (In the UK it is illegal to light fireworks after 11pm.)

✳ Never return to a firework after it has been lit, even if it looks like its not going to go off.

✳ Don't forget to wrap up warm! It's winter! It's COLD!

GALETTE DES ROIS

* SERVES 6-8
* PREPARATION TIME: 30 MINUTES
* COOKING TIME: 45 MINUTES

In France on Twelfth Night you eat Galette des Rois. It's a puff pastry tart that's filled with boozy frangipane, which is an almond cream, and sometimes with fruit. It is called King Cake, because in old folklore it was said to be the cake that was given to the kings who came to see Jesus. A crown is popped on it that someone gets to wear and the almond cream contains two figurines – whoever finds them gets to become king or queen for the day. Most of all though, I've included this recipe because I LOVE FRANGIPANE; I make mine a bit rounder in flavour with the zest of a lemon and an orange.

2 x 320g (14oz) packets of ready-rolled all-butter puff pastry

3 free-range egg yolks, lightly beaten

For the almond cream

75g (2¾oz) unsalted butter, at room temperature, plus extra to butter the baking sheets

75g (2¾oz) ground almonds

100g (3½oz) icing sugar

1 free-range egg

1 tablespoon dark rum or Cognac

a pinch of sea salt flakes

zest of 1 lemon

zest of 1 orange

½ teaspoon almond extract (optional – you can also use vanilla)

Using a plate as a template, cut a 20cm (8 inch) circle for the tart base from 1 sheet of the pastry, and a 22cm (8½ inch) circle from the second one. Place on buttered baking sheets and leave to chill in the fridge for 1 hour minimum.

Mix together the butter, almonds, icing sugar, whole egg, Cognac, salt, citrus zests and almond extract (if using) in a mixing bowl until it forms a smooth mixture and all the butter is incorporated. Keep in the fridge until ready to use.

Brush a 2cm (¾ inch) ring around the edges of the smaller circle of pastry with the beaten egg yolk. In the centre, smooth the almond cream into an even flat circle with a palette knife, taking it up to the egg-wash ring. Carefully place the larger circle of pastry over the almond cream, lining up the edge neatly. With your thumb, squeeze out any air and seal all around the galette. Brush the whole lid with beaten egg yolks (reserve the remaining egg yolks). Chill in the fridge for 30 minutes.

Preheat the oven to 200°C/180°C fan (400°F), Gas Mark 6. When ready to cook, remove from the fridge and brush with beaten egg yolks a second time. This will give the galette a really lovely glaze. With a sharp knife, start from the centre and score a spiral right up to the edge of the pastry around the entire lid, with the score lines about 5mm (¼ inch) apart.

Cook in the preheated oven for about 45 minutes, until the galette has risen and has a rich dark golden top. Serve at room temperature.

BREAKFAST CARBONARA

This is my dream hangover cure. Use whatever long pasta you want, but I like spaghetti or linguine. This recipe will make 200g (7oz) worth for 2 people – normally I'd serve 80g (2¾oz) per person, but we're hungover here, so you're having a treat.

200g (7oz) spaghetti

a dash of olive oil

120g (4¼oz) thick-cut guanciale (pig's cheek pancetta – get it from Italian delis), or pancetta or smoked bacon, thinly sliced

3 free-range egg yolks

50ml (2fl oz) single cream

40g (1½oz) Parmesan cheese, finely grated, plus extra to serve

a pinch of freshly ground nutmeg

sea salt flakes (the cheese and bacon are already salty) and stacks of freshly and finely ground black pepper

Bring a large pot of heavily salted water to the boil. This is where people get cooking pasta so wrong. The pasta needs to be able to have a proper little jig in the water, and it's seasoned heavily because you want the pasta to absorb the seasoning. Get the biggest pot you have, fill it with water and add as much as 1 tablespoon of salt. Your palate and body will thank you. When it's at a rolling boil, put your pasta in and cook it for about 1½ minutes less than the packet tells you to. Take a strand out and taste it. It should be seasoned and have a bit of bite to it. It will cook a little more in the sauce.

Meanwhile, heat the oil in a frying pan over a low heat, add your guanciale and fry until the fat is mostly rendered and the guanciale is nice and crisp and golden. In a separate bowl, beat together the egg yolks, cream, Parmesan, nutmeg and season with a little salt and plenty of black pepper.

When the pasta is ready, strain it, reserving about 50ml (2fl oz) of the cooking water. Toss the pasta with the guanciale and its fat, then quickly add the creamy, cheesy egg mixture with the reserved pasta water and mix quickly over a VERY LOW heat until the pasta is covered in a clingy velvety sauce. Divide the pasta between two plates and serve (with more grated Parmesan), and perhaps a Bloody Mary. Bingo! One very happy hangover.

INDEX

A

anchovy 69, 123
apple
  with cheese 207
  cider fritters 52–3
  in mincemeat 98, 99
  spiced cider 10–12
  in stuffing 172
avocado
  with corn cakes 224
  with enchiladas 211
  with frijoles 222
  with hash 216–17
  salad 137–8

B

bacon
  in carbonara 234–5
  pigs in blankets 196, 215
  on roast turkey 161
  in sour cream dip 116
  sprouts & chestnuts 190
  in stuffing 168–9, 172
  in tartiflette 227–9
beef, roast rib with mustard
    gravy 174–5
beetroot, pickled 120–1
blue cheese 65, 206
blueberry cobbler 77
bread sauce 195, 215
breakfast carbonara 234–5
bresoala 106
broccoli, ombrassica salad 122–3
Brussels sprouts
  bubble & squeak 219
  creamed 191
  ombrassica salad 122–3
  roast 191
  shredded salad 62–3
  with smoked bacon &
    chestnuts 190

sweet potato & corn
    hash 216–17
bubble & squeak 219
buffalo sauce 65
burrata, roasted 114–15
butter
  brown 76
  garlic 73
butternut squash, goose &
  pomegranate Thai salad 218

C

cabbage
  bubble & squeak 219
  red, with pomegranate 184–5
cake
  chocolate Christmas 81–3
  Devil's food cake 27–9
  ginger 198
  gingerbread latte 84–5
  Jewish cheesecake 94–5
  Yuletide log 90–2
capicola 106
carrots 44–5, 186–7
casserole
  chicken, chorizo & spelt 230–1
  sausage, tomato, lemon, caper
    & olive 42–3
  sausage hotpot & root
    vegetable mash 44–5
cauliflower 64–5, 122–3
celeriac, in mash 44–5
celery 65
charades 89
charcuterie board 106–7
cheese
  blue 64–5, 206
  burrata 114–15
  Cheddar, onion & potato
    hand pie 46–7
  goats' 120–1
  plate 204–7

ricotta 22–4
  in tartiflette 227–9
cheesecake, Jewish 94–5
cherries 31, 33, 82
chestnuts
  rosemary roasted 38
  sprouts & bacon 190
  in stuffing 168–9, 172
  Yuletide log 90–2
chicken
  chorizo & spelt casserole 230–1
  coq au vin pie 14–16
  crispy skin 119
  & girolle pithivier 130
  liver parfait 108–9
chocolate
  cake 27–9
  & caramelized chestnut
    Yuletide log 90–2
  chocolate-orange cream
    liqueur 152, 154
  Christmas cake 81–3
  malted hot 54–5
chorizo 230–1
Christmas crackers 171
Christmas Day 146
  countdown 150–1
  games 89
  laying the table 170–1
  playlist 177
Christmas Eve 126
  countdown 150
chutney 107, 207
cider 10–12, 52–3
clambake, New England 70–3
clementine 193, 194, 198–9, 215
cobbler, blueberry 77
corn see sweetcorn
cornichon 107, 132
court-bouillon 72, 113
crab, seafood platter 112

Author's acknowledgements

Firstly I need to thank the whole team at Octopus. To begin with, the person who makes this all happen is Stephanie Jackson my publisher. You gave me another book! Chuffed to bits about that. Thank you, but also thank you for being so honest, but always keeping the faith (and me in line). I hope I was a "little" less all over the place this time. Next, my editor, Sybella Stephens. You have a fantastic way with words and just seem to get me to get things done. I do believe the three of us are getting into a mighty fine groove. Thanks to Pete in production, Kevin in Sales, Caroline and Ellen in Publicity and Matt in Marketing.

Then we hit the art team. The Creative Director Jonathan Christie for being a brilliant sounding board. Thanks for always being so chilled when we were all manic, and sharing the same eye for detail and finish that I do. Emma Lee, your photographs are so beautiful. I fear too beautiful for "rough-around-the-edges" me. You have captured the magic of each of the festivities through your lens. You are so talented and kind and sweet and gentle and have no ego – a dream to work with. Anita Mangan, I have wanted to work with you since the beginning and I finally asked and asked and got. Let me tell you, you did not disappoint! What a bloody laugh you are. Sorry I change my mind so much and am so insecure about my ideas. You'd think by book four I'd be a whizz at this, but I'm not – you managed to draw it out of me and then draw it for me. Too many cats...? I DON'T THINK SO! Not when they have mermaid tails.

For the food team I have to thank Rose. Oh Rose. I don't even know where to start. You have gone above and beyond the call of duty. Picking me up off the floor when I'm down and dragging me down off the ceiling when I get too much into a whirl. There have been many moments when it has all gotten too much, but you have managed to keep me on my toes and draw the best out of me. Thank you for holding me up, making me look good when I don't deserve it and make me smile when I feel the world, heavy on my shoulders. You cook like a little pro and you should have an abundance of faith in yourself for this is a rarity. Thanks to the dream BABE that is Emily Ezekiel, my ingenious food stylist and your team Chrissy and Tamara. What a blast. I love working with you Emily. There's not much more to say than you are the best out there and I feel so spoilt that you want to work with me over and over again.

To my management team at ROAR Global: Severine, Jonathan, Kate and Ed. Another book. We've been working together for more than 8 years now. You guys always have my back and you know I love you all and value everything you do for me. The same goes for you at Beaumont Communications: Tim, Claire and gang. Thank you for always supporting me and always getting me fantastic PR in a very crowded world.

Now for my family. Jamie, thank you for being by my side and holding my hand through this. Two mad, passionate creatives living and working under one roof. I know I've driven you crazy some days making you try food when you've been in your musical bubble. Thank you for allowing my stuff sometimes needing to take first fiddle to yours, when you have a just as busy and "all-over-the-place" life as mine. Thank you for coming on the work trips and letting me have last-minute dinner parties and the 15 Christmases we had. Or even coming to the endless pop-ups and events when you should have been working on your own stuff. Thank you for the washing up, the glasses of wine and the chat and the music while I've been cooking for this book.

My mother Maria, again so many of these recipes are about you. I feel so proud for us as a family that I get the opportunity to spread your food around the world. Thank you once again for being the biggest inspiration and support. Sad we didn't have Spain this time... I'll work on it for next time. Heni and Cora – you two little legends. Thank you for holding my hand through all the troubles of the last year. I am the middle child and boy do I show it, but I get away with it with two power houses for sisters to hold me up. And you have lucked out with your boys, who are like my big brothers, Matt and Keiron. To Edie and Sholto for always making me smile. Edie I love that you and I are the same person. I watch you both grow with such glee. To my best friends Martha, Caroline, Laura, Zoe, Elly, Rosie, Neil, JD, Stephen and Dean, gaaah too many people to name. I just love my mates – you all know who you are. Thank you for listening and being patient with me. I hope it's all worth it.

xxx